Green
with
Envy

Green
with
Envy

Why Keeping Up with the Joneses
Is Keeping Us in Debt

SHIRA BOSS

WARNER
BUSINESS
BOOKS™

NEW YORK   BOSTON

Warner Business Books
Warner Books

1271 Avenue of the Americas, New York, NY 10020

The Warner Business Books logo is a trademark of Time Inc. Used under license.

Printed in the United States of America

First Edition: May 2006

10 9 8 7 6 5 4 3 2 1

Library of Congress Cataloging-in-Publication Data
Boss, Shira.
Green with envy : why keeping up with the Joneses is keeping
us in debt / Shira Boss—1st. ed.
        p.   cm.
ISBN-13: 978-0-446-57835-6
ISBN-10: 0-446-57835-5
1. Money—Psychological aspects   2. Finance, Personal—Psychological aspects.
3. Wealth—Psychological aspects.   I. Title.
HG222.3.B67 2006
332.024—dc22   2006002834

To Dad:
the best parent, teacher, supporter, and friend

∽

Acknowledgments

Everyone loves the idea of finding out what's really going on with other people's finances, yet few of us feel ready to spill our own secrets. This book is possible because some people were brave and generous enough to let me interview them in detail about their personal lives—in all cases, in much more detail than I included here—and share their stories with you. Most of the characters requested anonymity, so I use their pseudonyms in expressing my thanks.

My husband was the first to recognize the good intentions of the project and patiently allowed me to expose our private life. Over the following two years he indulged my consuming interest in the lives of the other characters, gave advice and encouragement, and was the first to read and comment on each chapter. Thank you so much.

John and Tina not only frankly laid out the inside story of their finances and their relationship but never questioned my need to pry into these matters. If I'd known how cool you'd be about it, I would have asked sooner!

Dan and Tammy let me into a part of their lives that they couldn't share with even friends and family. I'm grateful you stepped forward with your time and patience in the interest of helping other families.

Acknowledgments

Jack Quinn and Sam Gejdenson without hesitation agreed to be interviewed, given the aim of the book. Jack Buechner took the time and interest to educate me candidly about the inner workings of Capitol Hill. They and other unnamed former members of Congress took off the veil and admitted what really went on financially and emotionally while they were in office. Your trust and honesty are heartening.

Tucker made himself available for hours of interviews on a short deadline, and he shared insights about his life with impressive candor. I am awed at how you materialized out of millions of potential boomer characters and dozens of declined requests for help with this chapter.

Middy and Citizen Q not only hosted me in their home and gave me a behind-the-scenes tour of their world but were early providers of curiosity, advice, and encouragement about the book. I admire you both in many ways, especially for your generosity of spirit.

Thank you to the experts who gave their insights and assistance: psychologist Scott Wetzler, the Reverend Stephen Bauman, attorney Jan Baran, advertising authority James Twitchell, Brad Sagarin in the psychology department at Northern Illinois University, Sarah Phillips in the history department at Columbia University, Jerry Climer at the Congressional Institute, credit counselors George Janus and Howard Dvorkin, financial adviser Dave Ramsey and his assistant Beth Tallent. Thanks also to my Financial Peace University hosts, Rob Davis and Brother John Cortes, and classmates at Christ Tabernacle.

Jennifer Carlson, my agent, is a true gem. She has guided me from the beginning, patiently and thoughtfully helped me develop this book from the idea stage, and promptly read every word as it was written. Sincere thanks to Jen, Henry, Betsy, Rolph, and Irene at Dunow, Carlson & Lerner Literary Agency for their support.

I am especially grateful to Beth de Guzman and Rick Wolff, my editors at Warner, who enthusiastically backed this project from the very beginning and helped shape it into an even better product.

Acknowledgments

Thank you to Sam Freedman for his rigorous book-writing seminar at Columbia's graduate journalism school, and to my colleagues from that alumni group, especially Lindsay Pollock, Ivor Hanson, Sarah Richards, Dave Lawrence, Mitra Kalita, Phyllis Vine, and Michael Bobelian.

Among the editors I work for, Alex Sachare, Erik Ipsen, and Brent Bowers have been especially supportive and inspiring.

I'm blessed with friends who have given me company and counsel, kept me entertained, helped me weather frustrations, and held my hand through the book birthing process, in some cases giving feedback on outlines and chapters. I wrap my heart around Roya Babanoury (my one and only Ling Ling), Dina Cheney, Kendra Crook, Maria Ezpeleta, Adam and Kathleen Fifield, Chad Finley, Aina Lakis, John Madeira, and Mark Spellen. My friends and colleagues Lewis Taylor and Rebecca Nolan gave early contributions and inspirations. Liz Dribben has also been a persistent cheerleader.

The members of my family have believed in me wholeheartedly, given their support and encouragement in every way possible, and very patiently awaited this first book. My deepest love and gratitude to Dad, Mom, Murat, Debby, Erika, Jeff, Barbara, Julia, Anne, Baba, and Umut.

One final nugget, for readers who are book geeks like myself who peruse the acknowledgments as one way to learn more about book writing and publishing: If you want to develop a narrative nonfiction book, I highly recommend the book *Thinking Like Your Editor*, by Susan Rabiner and Alfred Fortunato. Then, to make sure the job gets done, turn to *The Clockwork Muse*, by Eviatar Zerubavel. Both have been indispensable to me.

Author's Note

The stories revealed in these pages are completely factual to the best of my knowledge. In order to protect personal identities, most of the characters' names have been omitted and pseudonymous first names used. The exception is Chapter 4, in which full, real names are used, or none at all.

Dialogue that was recollected appears in *italics*. If I heard it myself and wrote it down, it appears with quotation marks.

Contents

Green
with
Envy

CHAPTER ONE

✣

Green with Envy

It started even before the couple next door moved in. The comparison. The envy.

My husband and I live in a relatively small apartment building on the Upper West Side of Manhattan, where the gossip—the *news*, as it were—traffics in our cramped elevator or basement laundry room. Behind its thirty doors, our building houses a flutist, a filmmaker, lawyers (both corporate and public sector), interior designers, a nurse, an accountant, a grad student, an expatriate retiree who feeds the birds in Central Park, and the usual coterie of mystery inhabitants: They're around, even during the weekdays, they own cars (unusual in this area, where parking spaces start at $400 per month), they seem to be supporting themselves comfortably, but we're not sure how. The building has units from rectangular studios to penthouse two-bedrooms. Perhaps what sets the residents apart the most is how long each has lived here. Considering how real estate values have tumbled upward in recent years, the newcomers are consistently quite a bit better off than those of us already here. Five years after moving in, for example, our mortgage—the one we

1

stretched our debt-to-income ratio to the absolute outside limit to get — is about equal to what the down payment would be now.

In this environment, the most prized fruit of the grapevine is which apartment is being sold, and for how much. So when our neighbors right next door to us put their place on the market, you can be sure we were interested in who was moving in, and at what price.

And then we heard. In the elevator. The seller told me that a young couple our age was buying it — for over the asking price — and that they were paying cash.

Cash?

Somebody's daddy has some money! our neighbor guessed.

Yeah, I guess so. We couldn't imagine living mortgage-free at our age in Manhattan. And most of our friends couldn't imagine owning any property here at all. We had been the envy of our friends for having scraped together a down payment and bargaining our way into a mortgage. But hearing about our new neighbors, who would have no mortgage at all, we were the ones who felt kind of behind. And certainly mystified. We couldn't help but wonder where that kind of money was coming from.

There were two possibilities as to how the buyers accomplished this very large cash purchase, and my husband and I speculated about them at length. Either, as the seller thought, Mommy and Daddy helped them out by writing an enormous check (and that's how we referred to them, "Mommy and Daddy," as opposed to when our parents helped us out, in which case they were referred to simply as "our parents"); or they belonged to that dreaded class of twentysomething dot-com millionaires. We weren't sure which was preferable. Both seemed frustratingly undeserved.

We met. We had been ready to be annoyed by them, for them to be privileged, East Egg people, or intolerable hipsters, but actually John and Tina were very nice, apparently normal people. They seemed like a quirkily mismatched couple: Tina, a petite, brunette

Italian, had a stylish haircut and wore chic clothes surely from a downtown boutique. John, a taller, blond, we-soon-learned Upper West Side Jewish native, seemed more like a kindred spirit to me. He had just gotten out of a PhD program for geography (we got that bit of info from looking them up on Google) and dressed simply in jeans and flannel shirts. They seemed to go to work in the morning like everyone else. I had visions of becoming good friends and living like the two couples on the 1950s sitcom *The Honeymooners*, always dropping in on each other. We put their finances out of our minds. *None of our business*, we told ourselves.

Then on a Friday afternoon I ran into Tina waiting in the lobby of our building with a small (new, chic) suitcase.

Going away for the weekend? I asked.

Yeah, I'm just waiting for John to bring the car around. We need so many things for the apartment—we're going antiquing Upstate.

Antiquing? Who uses *antique* as a verb? I wondered. Does it mean the same thing as hitting flea markets for neat old stuff? Because I would have been fine with hearing that, but the idea of our young neighbors going on an *antiquing* spree—when, years after moving in, we were still waiting to buy something to cover our windows—reminded me instantly of their wealth, and that they could afford to do things differently.

After making smalltalk about antiquing, I turned to the elevator and pushed the call button, but I was interrupted by a question:

Can you recommend a good cleaning lady?

I froze. We all have different definitions of financial success, and mine is being able to afford a cleaning lady. I had a boyfriend once who lived in his parents' six-bedroom place off Park Avenue, with a live-in cook and a cleaning lady who spent every other day scouring the apartment. It was like living in a 5-star hotel, or what I imagined that would be like. Thick white towels were always folded and fresh. When you threw anything into any wastebasket, it blinked back at you from the bottom. Clutter never had a chance. Nor dust, nor dirty dishes. The best part was that my boyfriend never had to give any of these chores a thought. To my mind he dwelled in house-keeping nirvana: total comfort, zero effort.

My husband and I have had the usual "discussions" about keeping our home clean, and not even *clean* clean, but just keeping it from sliding into squalor. We've often ended up with the solution that if we paid somebody else to do the dirty work even now and then, we wouldn't have this tension. I've heard that solution from married people and read it in women's magazines: "Hire a cleaner. It'll save you hundreds in therapy bills!" But it has always felt financially impossible. Money that would go to a cleaner could be put toward a dozen more important things. Necessary things. *Later*, we end up saying, *when we have enough money.*

But our new neighbors, they evidently already had enough money, and they could afford a cleaning lady.

Rather than play along, I decided to confront the envy by just being frank.

No, I told her. *Actually, it's my dream to have a cleaning lady, though.*

Tina, being a nice person, tried to make me feel better by saying, *Yeah, it's been so long since we've had one.*

So what's changed recently? I wanted to know. Whence these cleaning lady funds?

I'm not proud to recount my conversation later with my husband. *Antiquing?* I mocked. *And who keeps a car in the city, anyway? That's ridiculous. It's cheaper to rent one whenever you need it. Insurance, parking, not to mention the cost of the car itself—what's the point of paying for all of that when you can hardly ever use a car here anyway?*

My husband's response was even more delicious. *Well, we know how they can afford it*, he said smugly. *Without a mortgage, we could afford a lot of extra things too.*

From then on, every expenditure we noticed — packages arriving seemingly daily from Bloomingdale's and Restoration Hardware, hiring someone to repaint their apartment, the installation of the antiques! — it was all dismissed as "mortgage money."

They are the Joneses, and we are not keeping up. However much we understand that we are not — *not*, under any circumstance — to covet our neighbor's anything or to attempt to keep up with the Joneses, we can't seem to help it. We are gripped by this involuntary urge, a drive to compare and compete that is ingrained, at least in Americans, if not all people.

We have been challenging ourselves to keep up with the Joneses for time eternal, even though it frays our nerves and is a quest without any destination. We know we shouldn't do it, we try not to, yet we find it irresistible.

It's not just that we want more for ourselves but that we specifically want more than, or at least as much as, what others have. That's how we know how much we deserve: It depends on what the other guy has. Since the days of Cain and Abel we have been bickering and jostling over who has the better lot. Wealth and well-being are largely a mindset, and how we're doing in relation to the company we keep is key to our contentment.

It would seem logical that the people we envy the most would be those at the top of the ladder, the rich and famous. It's true that we are fascinated by the wealthy and celebrities, and might fantasize about living their lives, but we are driven by just that, curiosity and fantasizing. We don't really expect that with enough hard work and some good luck we will end up with millions in the bank and our whereabouts splashed across the cover of *People* magazine. It might happen to some, but we don't count on it.

Who we truly envy are our closest peers. Psychologist Herbert

Hyman defined this phenomenon in 1942 in an article titled "The Psychology of Status." He said we compare ourselves within "reference groups" of those around us and who are similar to us. We look to our classmates, our co-workers, our siblings and our neighbors to see how we measure up and, secretly, who we must catch up with. The super rich and famous have too many variables for us to match, but those with similar backgrounds to ours, with similar advantages and opportunities, those are the people we believe we should be able to match. When one among us breaks away and does much better financially, we feel put down. We want some kind of explanation. Are they just smarter? Did they make better decisions? Why them and not us? Is this fair, after all?

Our visions of success are built on a scaffolding of comparison, and planked with envy. Envy is the only vice warned against in both the Ten Commandments and the Seven Deadly Sins. In Dante's purgatory, the closest rung to hell is pride, the second closest is envy. Manhattan therapist Anita Weinreb Katz describes envy like this: "You want what that person has, and you want to destroy the person who has it. It's a very primitive feeling."

It's not pretty. We're certainly not proud of it, and usually don't want to admit that we are in its jaws. That leads us straight into troublesome secrecy. The don't ask, don't tell policy of life that lets us live around other people. On the rare occasion that someone admits bald-faced envy, we nearly crumble with commiseration and relief. A treasured quote from writer Gore Vidal: "Whenever a friend succeeds, a little something in me dies." We can laugh that off as an artistic temperament, but when we're honest with ourselves we know that there is more there, that we suffer similarly, by letting our relative positions in our various groups affect our well-being, whether we mean to or not. So we can't help ourselves from quietly scoping others' situations, from private investigating to figure out what others have and, consequently, what we should have too.

Tina invited me over for a late-afternoon glass of wine, to get further acquainted. My *Honeymooners* plan was progressing. As we walked up the stairs to her living room, she asked me what I do and I told her I'm a journalist.

Really? she asked. She seemed excited by it, and I felt proud that my job impressed her. Then she announced, *I work for the* New York Times*!*

No way! I said, while I really did think to myself, NO WAY! A competitive mushroom popped out at me like an airbag. I might not care about her wearing better clothes, but when it comes to career I didn't need competition living next door, on staff at the *Times*. Forget the *Honeymooners*, that was two generations ago. Times were gentler. I wanted to go back down the stairs and ignore our new neighbors and their wealthy parents and paid-for apartment forevermore.

Instead, I kept up the conversation with a dry throat: *You're a reporter too? What do you cover?*

No, I work in Web development.

Oh, thank you, thank you, thank you. She is *not* a journalist! I do *not* have to read her articles in the paper, talk shop, or keep up in any way! What a relief. We can be friends again. Maybe I'll knock on the door to borrow half a cup of sugar one day. I even scoffed a little at Web development. *Boring*, I thought.

My relief was short-lived. By the time we reached the top of the stairs it came to me: Web development . . . the Internet . . . *dot-com millionaire.*

Everyone heard stories of twentysomething millionaires minted in the late 1990s. They couldn't be avoided. They were on television, they were on the covers of magazines, and there weren't just a few junior moguls, they seemed to be *everywhere*. The economy was shaken up like a snow globe, and money really did seem to grow on trees, there for the plucking. The idea of building up a career or business through years of hard work was actually mocked. People used to ask me what I was doing still writing for newspapers and magazines, those relics: Why didn't I get an Internet job?

Seeing our peers get enormously wealthy on stock options was, to say the least, irksome. We were just as smart and educated and ambitious—how was it fair that they were so much more successful financially? It shouldn't be any of our business how much money our cohorts make, or how they do it. Why *do* we chip away at clues, then, building a financial profile of our friends and figuring out where we fit on the scale?

In the United States, at least, where productivity is valued more highly than anything and is generally measured in dollars, this comparison and competition is inbred. It feeds the system. The drive to consume more, to have more and better things, and continually to raise our level of comfort, is stronger here than any other place on earth.

The American Dream itself—the novel system in which every one of us, regardless of background, is not only able but expected to move up, to do better and have more—is at its heart about competition. We're trained to gaze up one level from where we are and to aspire to get what those people have. Once we accomplish that much, we're looking up again. By cultural design, there is no end to it.

Setting our goals based on what others are doing goes even deeper than human nature. Fleas, for instance, do some keeping up with the Joneses of their own. They are the world's highest jumpers. When you put a population of fleas into a box and put the lid on, a few times they'll jump up and donk their heads on the ceiling. Pretty quickly, though, they learn to jump just as high as the ceiling without hitting it. Take the lid off and they still won't jump any higher—until a new flea moves into the box who doesn't know anything about the old lid. The new flea jumps to great heights. The others see it. Then they all start jumping higher again.

Climbing over the Joneses isn't only a social and financial phenomenon but an economic one. Moving up is our reward for hard work. Desire and envy are the engines that keep us going. Trade up. Earn more. Improve. This is what keeps our capitalist economy throbbing. So while we're told not to attempt to keep up with the Joneses, *tsk-tsk*, we're also shown that that is exactly what we should do. If we all minded our own business, if we were all content with our lot as it is, the economy would slow and our standard of living—which we measure, for the most part, in *things*—would tumble. "An economy primarily driven by growth must generate discontent," writes psychologist Paul Wachtel in *The Poverty of Affluence*. "We *cannot* be content or the entire economic machine would grind to a halt."

The trouble is that what's good for the whole is not necessarily healthy for us as individuals. As Wachtel describes it, "Our personal lives run aground on the perpetual generation of desire and discontent." Americans are working longer hours and earning more money than ever before, but the reward in terms of greater satisfaction with our lives has failed to materialize. A survey asked who in America feels they have achieved the American Dream. Among those earning less than $15,000 per year, only 5 percent agreed. What about among those earning more than $50,000, which is the top half of the American public? A near tie, at 6 percent. In the Bible a teacher says, "And I saw that all labor and all achievement spring from man's envy of his neighbor. This too is meaningless, a chasing after the wind" (Ecclesiastes 4:4). Keeping up with the Joneses puts us on a never-ending, stomach-yanking roller coaster. And we bring it on ourselves.

As soon as John and Tina got back from their tropical honeymoon, she quit her job at the *Times*. The economy was in the midst of a major slump. Nobody who had a job was complaining, or at least nobody was quitting. But that's what dot-com millionairehood was all about: You did what you enjoyed, you worked while it was exciting, and then whenever you felt like it, you walked away. And so she did.

She was in the right industry at the right time, that's for sure, my husband said with a sigh.

Contrasting our situation with theirs was painful. Tina talked about how they would soon start "popping out the kids." The idea of us having children ourselves, while attractive in theory, seemed practically impossible. We figured John and Tina probably did argue, like everyone, but they probably didn't argue about money stress, like we did. It wasn't the material goodies we grew envious of, it was the ease with which they seemed to be able to live. From the clues we collected, John and Tina seemed able to afford a psychological lifestyle that, to our disappointment, far surpassed ours. While our lives felt suffocatingly on hold while we straightened out our financial issues, our next-door neighbors, at our age, were living carefree, apparently enjoying life and each other to the fullest.

As for us, after meeting each other in the Middle East, we spent two years in a very long-distance relationship. A lot of our funds went toward plane tickets and phone calls. After we got engaged, one of us had to move. He earned enough as an engineer to support us in his country, but I didn't speak the language at the time, and even though I had worked there for several months it had been quite stressful. English wasn't a problem for him, though, and we figured his European degree and engineering background were marketable anywhere. He would relocate and look for a job as a management consultant. At that time the economy was booming; there weren't enough workers to go around. As one of my friends assured me, *Your nail salon woman could get a job as a consultant.*

Except it didn't work out that way. He started job searching at what turned out to be the very beginning of the recession. Rather suddenly, everyone seemed to be cutting back rather than hiring. He looked for work for a full year before starting something entrepreneurial.

This was far from a fun time in our life. The first and most obvious challenge was that we hadn't planned on living on one income for very long. Certainly not one journalist's income. Even a successful writer's income is not designed to support two people in Manhattan. We considered moving, but it seemed a drastic measure for what we thought was surely a temporary problem. Instead we budgeted, itself a challenge when there is not a regular paycheck to allocate. As I have often joked about being freelance, living paycheck to paycheck is especially hard when you don't know when, exactly, the next paycheck is coming. We stopped going out, and since so few New Yorkers entertain at home, avoiding going out meant we didn't see friends very often. We spent a lot of time sulking.

That led into the second problem: keeping up appearances. One does not set out actually to lie about unemployment or financial stress, but they're not polite or comfortable subjects. And since my husband had started a company and was no longer actively job searching, people probably assumed he was doing fine. For my part, I didn't want to complain to friends about us not having enough money because they would guess it was due to my husband—since I was still working as I had—and that felt like an invasion of his privacy. It's not nice to complain, even worse to blame. We are taught that financial problems are personal, and they are especially personal when they involve a third party not participating in the conversation.

So when people did ask how my husband's work was going, I found myself replying *Good!* With my family we kept matters equally oblique. They surely picked up hints that we weren't doing great (like when we mentioned we might just skip going home for Thanksgiving), but we didn't go out of our way to explain the situation and they didn't ask. Even in the twenty-first century, it is expected that a man, if not the sole support of his family, should contribute at least half of the household income. Even though there are alternative arrangements that are increasingly accepted, in general men who don't earn the socially prescribed amount have an element of shame to contend with that women do not experience. So I didn't feel entitled to disclose our details, especially since he had relocated halfway around the world specifically for our relationship. In the meantime, I endured some conversations like this one with my older sister. On the telephone, I complained vaguely about not being able to afford something, but she cut me off abruptly:

It must be nice to have two incomes, though!

I could have asked her what second income she was referring to, but instead I just sighed and hedged and hinted, common tactics when it comes to discussing money.

Well, I said, *it feels like supporting two people on one income.*

No kidding that's what it felt like, because that's what was going on. I just couldn't come out with the truth.

Privately, money was making our life miserable. I got itchy and irritable trying to work in a home office with someone else at home. He left when he could, but without being able to afford recreation, he resorted to wandering the streets or sitting alone in the park. It made matters worse that he had left his entire social circle behind to move here.

Determined to be responsible, we tracked our expenses in detail. But when we saw how much money we really needed to be making every month to cover our fixed and necessary expenses, we got depressed and stopped keeping track. Overwhelmed, my husband abandoned exercising and gained weight. I became a nagger. To keep pace financially, I took on more work than I could reasonably handle, and late at night, to get my mind off of the stress, I went to bed hiding behind the latest Harry Potter.

A couple of times I went trolling the Internet for some kind of support. Surely there had to be somebody talking about this kind of situation, about handling the social side of financial problems.

Wasn't there a money doctor out there who could make us feel better?

I had never before understood why money is the often-cited number-one reason for marital trouble and divorce. I had guessed it meant that couples, having two separate personalities, couldn't come to terms on how to handle the household money. Through experience, I realized that it is money itself, as a very real character in our lives—a companion that is as cranky, consuming, and irresistible as any lover—that causes the strife. It's the secrecy, the shame, the acting, the convoluted psychology of it all. We live in an ultra-open culture that freely shares our most intimate concerns— but rarely when they involve money. When it comes to the intersection of our personal finances and the orbit of the world outside our front doors, we are suddenly starved of the information that gushes on any other topic. I knew that other people were in our same shape, miserable because of their financial situations and even more so from the stress of covering them up, from leading a kind of double life. But how to communicate with those people? I couldn't even find them on the Internet, which meant that for all practical purposes we were indeed alone.

As for my friends, even though I was not direct with them about what was happening with us, I felt let down that they did not read between the lines and figure it out for themselves. I expected support and some kind of commiseration, even though their openly acknowledging the situation might have been embarrassing. In the meantime, their own endowments bothered me in a way they never had before: Every time a friend openly indulged herself, I was reminded that I couldn't afford to do so. I started wanting things I had never even wanted before, merely because I knew I couldn't have them.

The problem we grappled with that became the most damaging was the eventual rise of resentment. These were the first two years of our marriage. That we were being cheated out of what was supposed to be one of the most wonderful times in our lives frustrated me. *What did we do to deserve this?* I wondered. Through my gray-tinted glasses, every other couple on Broadway seemed to be having the time of their lives. I was sure that come Monday morning, each went off to their respective jobs, and when they got home they frolicked. I imagined their lives as cozy and romantic, not consumed by financial worries. *Everyone is enjoying life but us*, I convinced myself, even as I knew it wasn't really true. I laughed bitterly when I read an item in a women's magazine about how if a man earns less money than his partner does it often damages the couple's sex life.

In the midst of our angst, John and Tina, to our eyes, fit right into this carefree, honeymoon mold. So even though we had resolved to concentrate on minding our own business, Tina quitting her job to extract every second of joy out of life seemed to us like some sort of personal insult.

We were feeding our frustration with assumptions. If we had hunted down statistics and believed that they referred to just some of the people in our own circle, and if we could have heard them describe their own struggles, we wouldn't have felt so isolated.

In fact, we were far from the only ones living paycheck to paycheck. One survey reported that most households are doing so sometimes, most of the time, or always. The American Psychological Association recently reported a survey that showed money to be the number-one stress in our lives. The country as a whole owes $800 billion on its credit cards, making an average balance of more than $7,500 for each household if we divided up the debt among all of us. So some of that must belong to households right next to ours. Every year, the National Opinion Research Center asks people whether they are better or worse off financially than the previous year, and consistently, millions declare themselves worse off. In a recent survey, 78 percent of respondents said their debts were "making their home life unhappy."

We say we know that money doesn't buy happiness, but we don't seem to believe it. We want more, and the more we get the more we want. According to research presented in the book *The Overspent American*, "Among those making $30,000 or less, 81 percent said they would need less than 20 percent more income to be satisfied, while only 40 percent of those in the $75,000+ category would be satisfied with a 20 percent increase."

We certainly were not the only ones whose relationship was being strained by financial issues. We've all heard that money is the leading cause of problems in marriages. Some research on bankruptcy shows that couples who file for bankruptcy are at least twice as likely to file for divorce as the general population.

As for unemployment, the fallout it causes, ranging from temporary malaise to social and emotional implosion, is a shared experience but one that isn't discussed openly. "People who have lived through downward mobility," explains a book on the subject written by an anthropologist, "are often secretive and cloistered or so bewildered by their fate that they find it hard to explain to themselves, let alone to others, what has befallen them." Therefore most of us don't hear about it, don't understand it, and are never prepared for handling it.

My husband's and my problem, as it often happens, was larger than fretting over the personal side of our finances. We were equally, or perhaps more so, upset by contrasting ourselves to our better-off friends and neighbors. It doesn't make logical sense why we should concern ourselves with the financial situations of those around us. After all, they're not paying our bills and we're not paying theirs. Life is not a zero-sum game, with one person's gain having to be another person's loss. So we have no real reason *not* to be glad for another's success. Right? If only it worked that way. In fact, it does matter to us. And the more difficulties we are having, the more the success of others, frankly, aggravates us.

In our competitive, comparison-minded culture, relative success is what matters. So another person's gain really can feel like our loss. Economists refer to "positional goods," the things we buy that are meant to set us a notch higher than others who don't have them; and psychologists ponder "status anxiety," our worry that we are not keeping up with others. In measuring where we stand, relativity is everything.

Professors at Harvard and the University of Miami conducted a survey about income. They asked over 250 people whether they would prefer to earn $50,000 per year while those around them earned $25,000, or to earn $100,000 while those around them earned $200,000. More than half chose the first scenario, giving up having twice as much total money in order to have relatively more than others.

A more nuanced experiment showed even more strongly how important relative wealth is to us. Researchers in Britain set up a computer gambling game in which each player got 100 units of currency. The subjects played to increase their wealth, and as they played they could also see how well the other players were doing. Then a new level of the game was introduced: First some random players were given a 500 unit bonus, and then all players were given the ability to pay some of their own currency in order to "burn" other players and reduce the other players' wealth. In what came as a surprise to the researchers, the game became all about burning. The players who hadn't gotten the bonus immediately struck out against the newly rich. Although it hurt their own wealth, two-thirds of the players spent their own currency to bring the wealthier players down.

Another bit of Petri dish proof that we care all too much about how much money our peers have comes from a recent experiment conducted at Princeton. A series of two players were openly explained the terms of a game that would be played only once: One player was given ten dollars and had to make an offer of some amount of that money to the other player. If the other player accepted the offer, both players would get to keep their money. But if the other player refused the offer, then neither would get to keep any money. Rational behavior says that Player B would accept *any* offer, since doing so meant personal gain, while refusal of any amount meant getting nothing. But that's not what usually happened. When Player A's offer was seen as unfair (a piddling dollar, for instance), it was usually refused by Player B, leaving both players with zero. As one of the study's authors wrote, "Player B often gives up a smaller sum so Player A doesn't get a larger sum."

The awareness and concern over what other people have is an issue for us when we notice we have less, and also when we have more. When I lived in the Middle East I learned about the belief in the "evil eye." Everywhere you go in some regions, you are stared down by blue eyes, mostly flattened disks of colored glass. One hangs at the entrance to every home, from the rearview mirrors of taxis, and near a business' cash register. Cafe owners cement them into the sidewalks in front of their cafes, factory owners paint them on the sides of their factories. Small eyes are wired into the designs of jewelry, sewn on to the fringe of hand towels, glued to the tips of toothpicks. Recently they came up with a new way to get the eyes into their lives: melting them into the sides of tea glasses. *What*, visitors always ask, *is with the eyes everywhere?*

They are not the evil eye itself, they are warding off the evil eye. The evil eye is, essentially, envy. These people believe that if you enjoy good fortune, you'd better look out because others will envy you and you will attract negative energy. You'll be struck down. The thinking is similar to that of ancient Greece, when mortals were cautious about having too much fun or achieving too much success because the gods could get envious and bring them down. That is why modern-day business owners are especially careful to engage the talismanic services of the blue eyes. They want to do well, they certainly seek good fortune, but they don't want to *appear* to be doing well. The eyes help with that predicament.

At first I laughed this off as silly superstition. Now, however, having been through tough times and the emotional and social havoc they wreak, I am a believer in the evil eye. I don't know if blue charms help prevent it, but the evil eye itself—the destructive force of envy—seems very real. Maybe seeing the blue eyes everywhere helps people keep their own envy in check because they are constantly being reminded of it, that it is wrong and that they don't want it in their lives. As for myself I don't know if living among the eyes when we were under hardship would have helped me keep perspective, but, disconcertingly, what I saw happening during that time is this: When things were rolling along great for friends, I got glum. I didn't exactly wish them ill, but I didn't genuinely celebrate for them, either. And believing that life's cycle of ups and downs would spin around to everyone eventually did make me, very privately, almost shamefully, feel better.

Tina decided to launch a new career as an interior designer. *My mom has a really good decorator*, she explained, *and I've always been interested in it.*

She started taking classes at the same time my husband entered business school. The two of them commiserated about having homework; John and I commiserated about having to do the cooking while our spouses studied.

But on our side of the wall, our talk was not about how similar we were to our neighbors but about how aggravatingly different. When my husband was accepted to business school we nearly cried out of relief and happiness. We had decided that if he didn't get in, he would have to go back to his country and work there again for a while. Going back to school meant our taking on six figures of student loans and braving two more years on a single income, but it also meant we could stay together, and it meant—or we had to believe it meant—nearly being guaranteed a well-paying job after two years.

Tina, on the other hand, had voluntarily given up a well-paying job and was going back to school on a whim because she happened to be interested in it. To fill her idle time, apparently. To amuse herself.

Or so we figured. After a few months of classes, something shocking happened.

Okay, I was not deliberately eavesdropping, but our building has very thin walls. Really, everybody knows this. You don't have a conversation in the hallway or while waiting for the elevator if you don't want the neighbors in on it. Usually this is a drawback.

Yet Tina had, for some very odd reason, come up to her apartment talking on her cell phone, and rather than entering her apartment, she conversed in the hallway, right outside our doors.

And here's what I—inadvertently!—discovered: Things were not as they had seemed. As I heard what she told her friend, I was not only fascinated but guiltily thrilled.

We're paying $115 for cable. Say, $90 for our cell phones. Car insurance is, like, $120 a month. Electricity, a hundred bucks, about . . .

She gave the sympathetic listener (not meant to be me, mind you) a detailed inventory of their monthly bills and announced a grand total with alarm in her voice.

This kind of goody doesn't land at your doorstep every day— or, normally, ever. I quickly and shamelessly compared their tab to our own.

And that's before, you know, just living, she said with despair. She didn't know how they were making it, she reported.

The fact was, they *weren't* making it.

The worst part about comparisons is that we often make them based on misinformation. We try to keep up with the Joneses, then it turns out, as it did in our case, that the Joneses as we know them don't even exist. Even when someone does in fact have the money it looks like they have, which is often not the case, the funds do not add up to contentment. Among American households surveyed that earn more than $100,000 per year, 27 percent said that they did not have enough money to buy the things they "really need." That gives new meaning to the concept of *personal* finance. Our financial situations and what they mean to our personal lives really do depend on our individual circumstances, surroundings, and mindset. We cannot, even if we wanted to, step into somebody else's life and experience what appears to be so good about it. Whatever we thought we would enjoy of theirs—*if we only had what they have*—wouldn't be the magic bullet we envision.

We perplex ourselves over scenarios that are not even true. My husband and I had constructed the dossier of our next-door neighbors out of circumstantial evidence and what turned out to be misleading appearances. In the absence of hard information and honest explanations, we cobble together our own image of the lives of the people we know and to whom we compare ourselves. Even though we know, intellectually, that everyone has his or her own problems, truly believing that the couple next door, our co-worker, or better-off sibling doesn't really have it better than we do is another matter. Nothing, in my experience, gives greater comfort at these times of envy than recalling that *things are not as they seem.*

The day I overheard Tina's conversation, I couldn't wait for my husband to come home so that I could reveal the juicy gossip of The Real Situation Next Door. We had gone wrong somewhere in our analysis. Tina was apparently not a dot-com millionaire after all, not a lady of leisure. And, mortgage or no mortgage, they *did* have money worries like the rest of us. We had heard them complain briefly about various expenses before, but we hadn't taken them seriously. After all, the more money someone has, the more they seem to feel obligated to complain publicly about high costs. (I had seen this in my Park Avenue boyfriend. When we opened the menu at an expensive restaurant, he would announce, *Twenty-eight dollars for pasta—who are they kidding?!*)

On the surface it was gossip, but on a deeper level, learning of our neighbors' troubles was significant to us because we had come to feel so achingly alone in our bleak financial world. Just as we had read into their having a fully funded, joyful life together, now we could project that just as we sometimes lost sleep over money, so did they. We no longer felt singled out for suffering financial stress at the beginning of a marriage. We had some proof that a couple just like us could be in a somewhat similar situation, even though it didn't look like it from the outside.

However, rather than commiserating—how could we, given that we weren't supposed to know their problems anyway—I gleefully recounted the entire scene to several friends: *You know our next-door neighbors without the mortgage? Listen to this . . .*

Some information and honesty go a long way toward curing the comparisons that ail us. If we would only talk to one another about money and status, about our desires and discontent. If only it were okay to reveal what really goes on in our financial lives, not just factually but emotionally, how much better off we would be. Truth is healing. Like having daylight return after a night spent worrying in the darkness, constructive confessions can banish our loneliness and soothe our financial fretting. How much damage we do ourselves by hiding our money misgivings, and how unnecessary this collective burden is. Our financial and emotional welfare depend not on earning more or owing less but on opening up and coming to understand the reality of those around us. The Joneses lose their power over us when we get to know them and understand what their own lives are really like, behind what is usually a tightly closed door.

How much better could my husband and I have felt if we had known the details of what was going on with the money next door, let alone with a few other people? Much. I can say this because I went investigating—prying, even—to figure out a few Joneses and solve our compulsion to keep up. I started by knocking on our neighbors' door and spending some time truly catching up with the Joneses. From there I went deeper into America, from suburbia to the nation's leaders and across generations. And just to make absolutely sure that money doesn't solve our problems, I got to know a billionaire and heard what most of us never know about that world.

You are about to learn the intimate details of what has been called America's last secret.

CHAPTER TWO

⌒

The Money Next Door

What was going on with the money next door was another version of the hiding and struggling that was going on behind our door. We just never knew it about each other.

I didn't get all of the details right away, of course. I had to ease into it. Even though I ask questions for a living, it is, shall we say, not normal or acceptable to knock on your neighbors' door and ask them what's been going on with their money. But I did it. For me and for you. Because I know you've been wondering about your neighbors too. And if I can show (which I will) that things are not as they seem, we might all stop paying envious attention to what other people have—or seem to.

I called Tina from my side of the wall and asked if I could come over for a chat.

"Yeah, the door's open!" she said.

I slinked over there.

She was a few months' pregnant and had quit her job—again. How smoothly their plan seemed to be progressing: starting to "pop out the kids," as she had said they would. She was reclining on the couch with a day-by-day pregnancy notebook. It seemed so luxurious to me, staying home with an entirely silent child and reading. And here I came, to ask about their finances.

Well, I didn't put it that way, exactly. Since we were neighbors and friendly, I used the excuse that I was researching an idea for a book about the social side of money and wanted to talk to people about it. All of that was true; I just didn't tell her yet that she and her husband held a special spot in the story. I told her how I had been inspired by hiding some of our own financial stresses.

I didn't have to say any more.

"Money is, by far, my number-one stress," she declared.

That first meeting I got a very general picture of their issues, but I didn't ask specifics. She said that she and John have very different attitudes toward money: She had been raised in the materialistic suburbs and described herself as "practically a compulsive spender." He, meanwhile, had been "raised by a Marxist and can live on practically nothing. That causes major problems." They couldn't live on her husband's salary, so her parents helped support them. (Even though her father, an accountant, thinks of her as a failure, she said, for not being able to manage money.) They couldn't afford the trip they were taking to Paris that weekend, but they were going anyway. As far as the luxury of not working went, she explained that now that she had quit her job, she realized how much our society defines everyone by what they do for a living, and she dreaded people asking her the question. She couldn't wait for the baby to be born so that she would have a legitimate occupation.

Soon after that conversation, Tina and I were walking into our building together and stopped to pick up our mail in the lobby. We both read the label on a box from Bloomingdale's before we saw that it was for her. She snatched it up, groaning, "Oh god, you're seeing what a spender I am."

She was right that I had a different perspective on the string of packages arriving for them after I learned that her spending was an issue between them. But still I did not pick up on her hints that the problem in their household went deeper than her just being a dedicated shopper.

The next discovery came over lunch. We were chatting about banks, and Tina mentioned that they use a certain bank because their mortgage is through that bank. *Mortgage?!* Our envy of these neighbors had been touched off years before when we heard that they had paid cash for their apartment. Now I found out that was incorrect information? (*Was it possible the rumor mill was . . . flawed?*) This whole time they were making mortgage payments after all? Two sentences later she mentioned having to keep their checking account at this bank because by doing so they had gotten some of the interest knocked off their home equity line of credit. *Home equity line of credit?!* I was too stunned to admit to her that we had heard they hadn't carried a mortgage and had been envious.

Tapping a home equity line of credit, I marveled to myself. Even my husband and I, with one income and graduate school tuition, had not resorted to that. I left my husband a message on his cell phone: "I just had lunch with Tina. You're not going to believe this! See you tonight."

At night we continued speculating. What was really going on over there? Had their parents helped them get the apartment by paying cash, but then John and Tina had to pay them back? Or, worse, had they accepted the gift of an apartment, only then to turn around and take a mortgage on it for extra cash?

Shame on us for caring. Yes, I know. I *know*! At least I'm being honest (here). And I know we're not the only ones who have conversations like this. The point is that for anybody who has ever had even an itch of wanting what their friends or associates have, it is most useful first to understand what it is they do have. Or, as the case may be, what they do not have.

After I received a contract for this book I asked John and Tina if

I could officially interview them about their personal financial life. Surprisingly, they agreed, and so I got to find out the real deal about next door.

Let's start where it all started for us: how they paid for their apartment. It was neither an Internet fortune nor purely a parental handout but, rather, something we never would have guessed: John paid for most of it himself, out of an inheritance he had received in college from his grandfather. *John, son of the Marxist, was the one with the money?* Of course we hadn't figured that one out. Neither have their close friends. "Our friends must wonder how we can afford to live here, knowing that I work at a nonprofit and Tina's not working," John said a little slyly. When money does come up in conversation with them, he said, "We don't tell the truth about it."

So John had some family money. (Even though the whole family looked very modest. His grandfather was a shopkeeper in Brooklyn who never spent a dime he didn't have to and quietly amassed a fortune through decades of making steady investments in the stock market.) John kept the nest egg in a brokerage account and only spent some of the income for travel. Having some financial security right out of school meant he could get a PhD and not have to chase a high-paying career.

When John and Tina decided to move from a rental into our building, their strategy was to convert the stocks to real estate by paying mostly cash for their apartment. That way they wouldn't have a mortgage and could live on a smaller income. Her parents did contribute, but not on the magnitude we had assumed. They gave them about 15 percent of the cost of the apartment. After they closed, John and Tina took out a mortgage for about 10 percent of the apartment's value in order to restore some of the nest egg and free up some cash.

The antiquing spree? Her parents "chipped in," as they put it, to pay for new furniture as a housewarming gift. Okay, that was nice of them. What about the kitchen and bathroom renovations? That was done economically, they insisted, with John's dad doing some of the installation, and the materials paid for out of a home equity line of credit. *The home equity line of credit!*

Through all of this questioning—a dream come true in terms of being able to get the facts for a change rather than speculating and surmising—there was one thing, personally, I was eager to hear about: *the cleaning lady*.

Tina: "Well, we both hate to clean."

John: "*You* hate to clean."

Tina (with an eye roll): "It wasn't getting cleaned."

So far, so normal. It sounded like they'd been having the same "Why isn't the house clean, and how are we going to get it clean?" talks on their side of the wall as we had on ours. But the *money*. If they somehow had been choking on their budget just as we had been, how did they justify paying for help?

When they first moved in—when Tina asked me for a cleaning lady recommendation—they were both working. With the apartment purchase, their monthly housing cost, including the minor mortgage and the maintenance payment, dropped to about half of what they had been paying in rent. They could, therefore, afford the services of a cleaning lady. "Financially we were doing great," Tina said. Then she added, "For a short time."

My interviews with John and Tina were juicy. Satisfying. Imagine what it would be like for you to walk up to anybody you have envied or secretly competed with or wondered about and outright ask them the bare truth. The details. To reconcile your impressions of them with the full-blown reality of their lives.

Now picture the other side. What if someone came up to *you*, and wanted you to open your books, to disclose not only every number of your household finances but to reveal what thoughts you have had, what comparisons you have made, to explain how any issue related to money has ever gnawed at you.

For most of us, finding out about others would be most exhilarating, while having to come clean ourselves would fall somewhere between distasteful and mortifying. That's because, as has been pointed out again and again without anyone being able to do much about it, money is—gasp, whisper—*taboo*. In psychology circles money is given even higher hush status as the Last Taboo.

It used to have more company. The list of topics generally deemed off-limits for public or even private consumption a generation or so ago included illness (cancer, in particular), death, and sex. Mental health used to be nobody's business but your own, but that has certainly changed in recent years, when comparing prescriptions for antidepressants has become an accepted topic of conversation. A friend of mine speared two former taboos at once when he complained to me—in the middle of a crowd of his co-workers—that taking Prozac was killing his sex drive.

The age when married couples on television sitcoms slept in separate beds has long since past. For that matter, thanks to the breeding of afternoon talk shows, the time when people who committed adultery with their friends' spouses kept that information off national television is apparently gone too. An editor I met for the first time, who was in agreement that money reigns over a final zone of secrecy, blurted out when we were discussing what's left *not* to be discussed: "I used to think sex with animals was the last taboo, but now that's out the window!" (*It is?* Well, anyway . . .)

A recent cover story in *Money* magazine, "Secrets, Lies and Money," showed the results of their survey of 1,001 adults with household incomes above $50,000. What scenario would they find most uncomfortable? one question asked. Their guests seeing their bottle of the impotency drug Viagra? Fifteen percent chose that as supremely embarrassing. Guests seeing their pay stub or tax return? More than twice as many respondents chose that, at 34 percent.

In introducing a week of articles focused on money, *Salon* called money "our totem and fetish object." The Reverend Stephen Bauman, a preacher in New York City, said in his Sunday sermon recently—after one mention of Christ, two mentions of Jesus, one mention of Viagra, and six mentions of sex—"There is one last taboo, one last holy of holies in our private lives, one secret arena that is too personal, considered too impolite for sharing: that's our financial situation." A psychologist who has researched money's effect on our relationships wrote in a professional journal, "The money taboo is a serious psychological problem because, though we do not talk freely about money, it is of major concern to almost everybody in America." Or, as a journalist friend of mine put it, "Everyone wants to know, but nobody wants to tell."

The same goes for having money, and being out about that. "There's a code of silence about wealth that you're not supposed to break," said Jamie Johnson, a young heir to the Band-Aid company fortune who made a documentary film about children of very wealthy families. Not only did he have a lot of trouble recruiting subjects for his film—most people wouldn't talk, and others who did later said they regretted it, while one even sued—but Johnson himself has been shunned by some of his wealthy peers for being a "traitor." Among the insults: no more invitations to debutante parties. "I guess I used to be considered an eligible bachelor," he said. "But not anymore." After all, who would want to welcome into their family someone so uncouth and slippery as to talk openly about money?

I wanted to deconstruct this taboo and try to figure out where this destructive nonsense came from. The most basic building block of the money taboo is plain manners. Social custom. We're taught from a young age, usually by example but sometimes outright instructed, that money talk is just not polite, so we shouldn't do it. I have on my reference shelf, I'll admit, the hefty sixteenth edition of *Emily Post's Etiquette*. When I went to see what it had to say on the topic of discussing money, I found that, like popular culture itself, the book had more to say about sex. In the chapter "Your Personal Life," readers are instructed: "Lovemaking is a personal matter that does not belong in public. Displays of affection or attraction are often embarrassing to others, are not appropriate in the presence of children, and belong in a private setting. In this country, holding hands, affectionate greetings accompanied by a kiss on the cheek, or a quick hug are perfectly acceptable in public. Passion is not."

When it comes to money, though, only two scant lines are listed in the index: "gifts of" and "as wedding gifts." But with some digging, I found *tsk-tsks* against discussing finances under other headings. In a section on "Good Neighborliness" it is pointed out that, "Just as you would be appalled to hear someone talking about your financial difficulties, another would be hurt to hear you gossiping about hers." (Oops.) But wait: When would we or our neighbor have learned about our respective financial difficulties? The only other mention of talking about money—and this book does actually cover how to have a conversation and what to write in friendly letters—is under the heading "Snoops" and addresses how to respond if someone asks how much something of yours cost. "Inquiries about money matters are usually in poor taste and should be given short shrift. You cannot say, 'None of your business,' but you can say, 'I'd rather not talk about that, if you don't mind. With the cost of living what it is, the whole subject is too depressing . . .' and change the subject."

Change the subject. That does sum up what has evolved as common sense on the matter. But why? Why are we so afraid of discussing money? Where does the money gag come from? And why can't we shake it, even in the reign of the Information Age?

I went looking further back, to the Bible. Scripture has plenty to say about money, wealth, poverty, making money, giving money away, what is virtuous about having money, and also how love of it can be our downfall. Jesus, by example, talked quite openly about finances, both his own and others'. "Interestingly, and tellingly, of all the words ascribed to Jesus in the Gospels, one-sixth of them pertain to money—the only subject he speaks about more is the King-dom of God," said the Reverend Bauman in his sermon on—*his* title, not mine—"The Last Taboo." Bauman confirmed for me that there's nothing in Scripture about keeping our financial lives to our-selves. Yet even in his position as a minister, he doesn't get congre-gants consulting with him on the issue of money, even when it comes to tithing or charitable contributions. "Almost never," Bau-man says. "They'd be much more prone to discuss *any* issue or problem than their finances."

In another sermon about money, similarly entitled "The Taboo," the minister of a church in Toronto gave this explanation about our inhibitions:

> Why is money so difficult to talk about? Because when we talk about money we are never talking just about money. Money we come to believe is a reflection of a person's value. You have it and you're good, you don't and you're not, or at least not as good as. On the other hand some people feel embarrassed by how much they have or, having it, are wary of being taken for what they have . . . "So please let's not talk about it so I don't have to deal with the feelings I have about money—wariness and fear, the anger, the embarrassment and shame."

Psychologists have come to similar conclusions. But not, I must say, as far back as Sigmund Freud. Not to gossip about a great thinker, but Freud was kind of the original sinner when it came to whitewashing money talk. Although he had a lot to do with breaking the sexual taboo, he actually contributed to building up the money taboo. In a 1903 essay, he described money's legacy of being dirty: "In the ancient civilizations, in myths, in fairy tales and supersti-tions, in unconscious thinking, in dreams and in neuroses—money is brought into the most intimate relationship with dirt." He points to "ancient Babylonian doctrine" as equating gold with shit and goes on to explain that a child's fascination with his own excrement can carry over into adulthood by becoming a fascination with money.

That much is about what we would expect from Freud. The really interesting part is when we turn the looking glass on Freud's own private life. In his personal correspondence he points to money as his biggest concern. When Emma Jung, the wife of Freud's fellow psychotherapist Carl Jung, asked Freud about his interpretation of his own children's dreams, Freud told her he hadn't done any analysis of them. Emma wrote to him, recalling their exchange, "You said that you didn't have time to analyze your children's dreams because you had to earn money so they could go on dreaming."

And he had other issues. As psychologist Richard Trachtman points out, "Referring to his father's financial setbacks, [Freud] admitted that he preferred to suppress rather than explore their impact on him. About the 'hard years' he wrote, 'I think nothing about them was worth remembering.' This is a striking statement for a man to whom exploration of traumatic childhood memories was a linchpin of early psychoanalysis."

Freud's turning his back on money—after portraying it as the lowest dirt—paved the way for about three generations of therapists who hardly looked into their patients' money issues. So even in a professional setting, an artificially safe environment designed for us to bring to the surface our problems and solve them, the money taboo has remained strong and counterproductive.

As I faced down the money taboo and interviewed John and Tina, the picture was somewhat coming together. And, frankly, it really did look pretty cushy. Not many people, certainly not many sons of leftists, can write a check for their first home, especially not in their twenties. That does seem certifiably enviable. But fine, some people do inherit a stack of money, and there's nothing the rest of us can do about it—except not assume that inheriting a nest egg means a carefree life.

With so much money flowing in from their families, one might naturally start to think, as we had, *It must be nice to be John and Tina!* But there was more to it, and when I learned the rest of the story, my envy pretty much evaporated.

More about our supposed lady of leisure, Tina: Her family gives her money, her husband has money. What is she *talking* about, money is her number-one stress?

She is an only child who has been spoiled her whole life. Yet she's not entirely thankful. "There's a reason it's called being 'spoiled,'" she said. Having everything she's ever wanted handed to her (albeit with strings attached) killed her ambition, as she tells it. Not that that's true of everyone whose parents are generous with them. Tina, for example, has always compared herself to and envied her cousin of the same age. Tina's uncle, a real estate tycoon, gave his daughter a lot, just as Tina had been given a lot by her father. But the uncle did it differently. He involved his daughter in his real estate business early on, taught her how the transactions worked, and eventually let her manage a small portfolio. Tina's father works more on the hand-out system, with doses of meddling. *You can have anything you want*, he tells her. *Just tell me what it is and I'll get it for you.* So things have materialized in her life, but she has never managed money. Tina has watched her cousin grow into a successful business owner, while Tina hasn't been able to settle into a career or build any wealth herself, which makes her feel incapable. "I never had to work for anything," she said. "My life ever since college has been a struggle about 'What am I going to do with my life?'"

Remember how it looked to us when Tina quit her job at the newspaper and went to interior design school? Here's what really happened:

Tina was miserable at her job. She found spending every day at a computer tedious and boring. It felt like drudgery. The upside was that she was making over $60,000 per year—nearly twice as much as

John—and for the first time in her life had managed to save money regularly, about $500 per month. Her dad for once trusted her enough to hand her some assets, and she had about $20,000 in a stock brokerage account.

They were feeling secure financially. John and Tina sat down to figure out whether they could afford for her to quit. John looked over the numbers—he was always the one handling the finances—and said that it would be very tight, but they could manage it. Of course the frugal one felt they could live on less. He didn't acknowledge how different his wife was.

Tina knew. In her gut she knew that tightening the financial belt was going to be a cinch that would only come undone.

She gave her notice to her boss anyway. She thought it would be a huge relief, to be free of her job. But it wasn't. *What am I going to do with my life?* she wondered. And then there were thoughts of the money. Tina didn't like the idea of cutting back their lifestyle, getting rid of cable and not being able to buy new clothes. Within a few days of quitting, while she was finishing up her last two weeks of work, she went back to her boss. She told him she had made a mistake and that she wanted her job back.

No.

It was too late to change her mind. Tina returned to her desk and sat there in a panic. *What about her career?* she wondered. What about making money? Then something hit her: *If I want to keep my job and my boss says no, then I was just fired.* She went to the human resources department and applied for unemployment. That income would help tide them over until she figured out what else to do, she thought. With the unemployment checks, and $500 per month given to them by her parents since she "lost her job," and with her parents paying her health insurance, John and Tina were getting by financially. But staying at home wasn't the luxury she had thought it would be. She was bored. She felt guilty. She wanted to be productive and find work she enjoyed, plus she still wanted to earn an income.

This was late in the summer before my husband started business school. That's when we heard that Tina was going back to school herself to learn interior design.

She was trying to make something of her life. She wanted to have a job she wasn't miserable at and to earn her own living. Having gone through many years of graduate school, John said he could hardly refuse to support her going back to school. And her father made them an offer: Finish the program, and he would pay back the tuition. In the meantime, they increased the home equity line of credit by $25,000 to pay for the classes.

She didn't finish. After the first semester, when she heard that her classmates were blasting résumés to all of the city's best interior designers, Tina did the same. After interviewing with one of the town's most talked-about designers, she was offered an entry-level job. It paid $30,000 per year, less than half her former salary, but the position was considered a great starting point in the industry, even had she graduated with a degree. "It was a dream come true," she said. Even if that's not how it turned out.

The designer worked for famous people and society ladies. His job was to decorate or redecorate their homes with the most extravagant furniture, fabrics, and finishes they could cull from the corners of the world. As Tina put it, "All of his clients had shitloads of money." For some reason—the combination of hearing "ladies" and lots of money, I guess—I pictured these clients as older women, divorcées or widows perhaps, with large-gem jewelry hugging sun-spotted skin. Not the case. Unfortunately for Tina, the clients were our age, in their thirties. They were not only young but beautiful. And stylish. *Stylish*!

Among the jobs taking place in Park Avenue residences and Greenwich Village townhouses, there was one client in particular. Not only close to Tina's age but exactly her age. A full-time socialite with a family fortune listed on the *Forbes* 400 list of wealthiest Americans. She ordered "Louis Quinze" chairs, as they called them, and for the color scheme of one room she told the designer she was determined to match the shade of cream a friend had used in his European residence.

Tina was sometimes alone at the client's home, to do things such as make sure the flooring guys laid down the carpet in the right room. She ventured into the woman's bedroom, through to the dressing area, and straight to her closet. Or closets, rather, as they lined the room. Inside, she encountered a section of perfectly hung jeans that stretched across four feet of a rack and other garments and shoes from top designers: Oscar de la Renta, Marc Jacobs, Manolo Blahnik. Not just ready-to-wear pieces but also the high-end collections. Couture. Outfits photographed on runways and featured in magazines. Tina could hardly fathom owning such a trove of fashion.

Then there was the storage room. In there, Tina saw racks and racks of similar clothing that the woman didn't wear anymore, that was to be gotten rid of somehow.

On the days Tina came face-to-face with the client, it was to drop off a package of fabric samples or hand her paint chips. "I was basically a gofer," she said. "I felt totally inferior."

She still made an effort to compete. "I did everything I could to be their equal in the presentation of myself," she said of the wealthy clients. She kept up with manicures and made sure she was creative with her hairstyles. But most of all she agonized over her outfits. She wanted to look *impeccable*.

Tina had always paid attention to fashion and was often shopping for new clothes and shoes, but now she ratcheted up her obsession. At Bloomingdale's she lost herself in the designer boutiques. She went to Barney's, New York's high-end department store. And she riffled through the chic shops of SoHo, near the office where she worked.

She was in search of the ultimate pair of jeans, unusual T-shirts, trendy handbags and classic coats. When she targeted an item, she didn't buy impulsively. She kept it in mind. She visited it again, tried it on. After three or four passes, if she was sure, she acquired it.

At first she dipped into the $7,000 savings she had built up when she was working at her last job. She used a credit card, which she wasn't supposed to have, and used her savings to pay off the bill.

She wasn't supposed to have the credit card because she had run up debt on it before. Repeatedly. In college she would buy clothes with the credit card and build balances of $5,000 or $6,000 that she couldn't pay off. As a Christmas or birthday present, her dad would pay off the balance. Then she would start over.

When John and Tina were looking to buy their apartment, John didn't want their credit reports showing any debt. When he found out Tina was carrying a $9,000 balance on her card, he clipped away some of his inheritance to pay it off. Then he ceremoniously cut up her card and made her agree not to use a credit card again. He thought that was the end of it.

Tina had planned for that to be the end of her charging, too. But just when she was burning through her savings shopping for clothes, a copy of the card, which she had forgotten she had, resurfaced. She furtively tucked it into her wallet.

For her job she was often running errands around New York, and she started stopping off to shop in between destinations. She developed a regular circuit and got to know all of the stores' inventories so that she could spot new arrivals in minutes. Within a twenty-four-hour period she would hit all three Barney's locations. On her lunch hour, instead of eating, Tina would go through SoHo shops, buy a couple of items, then pick up lunch on her way back to the office and eat it on the run or at her desk. When she got home, she would hide the packages in the back of their closet hoping John wouldn't figure out how much she was spending.

Her favorite shop became Marc Jacobs, the store of the designer whose creations lined the closets of the client she most envied. Tina was constantly in the store. She didn't invest in any exclusive Collection items but felt she could afford the ready-to-wear Marc by Marc line. The favorite price in that shop was $198. Or $298 for, say, a sweater. One by one, day by day, she collected much of the Marc Jacobs spring collection and then, over the summer, almost all of the fall collection: skirts, dresses, sweaters, and coats; $198, $198, $298 . . .

Not only were her $7,000 savings gone, but she had whittled away the money her dad had given her in the brokerage account. Every purchase was eventually going on The Card. It made her nervous, knowing she couldn't repay the balance. At home, before John got back from work, she would log on to her credit card account online and constantly check the balance. When a statement arrived in the mail she made sure to grab it before John saw it. *I'm done*, she would promise herself when she looked at the balance. *No more charging*. But then she would spot one more gorgeous item in a shop and say, *I have to have that.*

That was the summer my husband was still in school. All I saw was Tina looking fabulous. One morning we ran into each other in the hallway and walked to the subway together. She had her dark brown hair twisted into two short braids and wore a 1950s-style circle skirt with strappy sandals.

Wow! I told her. *You look so cute!*

Next to her I felt like a frump.

By August, Tina's shopping bills were ringing up at more than $1,000 per week, all on credit. She wore enough new clothes in front of John that he started to question what she was doing. *Is that new?* he was constantly asking her. She shrugged and kept telling him she was just getting a few things for her fall wardrobe.

Once John captured on TiVo a short segment on the local news about addictive shopping. He recognized some of the symptoms in Tina, such as when she found something she wanted she couldn't rest until she acquired it. He sat her down one evening and told her she needed to watch it. She was wiggling in her seat but insisted to John, *That's not me.*

They weren't spending much time together. John was busy training for the New York marathon, which meant getting to sleep in the evening and rising early to run. Tina was spiraling further into her funk and escaped into nights out late with her friends, getting drunk on rounds of rum-drenched, $8 mojitos.

In the thick of Tina's self-esteem crisis, a new woman was hired at the interior design firm: a six-foot-tall, blonde former model. A month later Tina was fired. She didn't even consider going back to any kind of work in interior design. She downplayed losing her job to her friends, explaining she had been preparing to quit anyway.

Nobody knew about her debt, even the girlfriends she was usually so close to. They saw her drinking heavily, though, and guessed she was down. One convinced Tina to go to the therapist the friend had been seeing. They set up back-to-back appointments on Wednesday nights, after which they would go to the friend's apartment, drink too much red wine, and gripe about their lives. Tina groaned that she "had debt and felt like shit." She didn't explain further. And her friend never asked.

At therapy, although Tina's secret credit card debt was weighing on her, along with her career crisis, session after session went by and she didn't bring it up. The therapist knew that money was an issue for Tina, because she had gotten a reduced rate due to financial hardship. Yet money as a topic wasn't directly addressed by the therapist or the patient. When Tina finally did come out with the problem, it took the whole hour for her to reveal the actual total of how much she owed. When the therapist heard it, she yelped, *Ti-na!*

That money is discussed at all in therapy is somewhat rare. The same taboo that stops the general public from addressing money openly often makes therapists themselves equally squeamish about it. "The social norm is so strong against discussing it. It just feels like financial voyeurism," says a therapist in Manhattan. I haven't heard of gynecologists or other doctors having invasion-of-privacy issues when it comes to treating their patients; how can the influence of money in someone's life be considered out of bounds for talk therapists?

Even when it comes to the doyen of therapy—the 12-step programs—the subject of money grinds confession to a halt. In a *New York Times Magazine* article, writer Carol Lloyd points out that while in other 12-step programs, participants are "expected to declare the worst about themselves—'I'm an alcoholic!' or 'I am a sex addict!'—Debtors Anonymous allows reticent members to introduce themselves, 'I'm Carol and I'm vague about money.' The question is, are we allowed to be anything else?" Lloyd describes her experiences further:

> Recently I was in a therapy group that put a premium on unexpurgated revelation. "Be specific," the psychologist urged us. "We don't want miscommunication." One day, a doctor in the group began worrying aloud about taxes. "How much money are we talking about here?" I burst out, unable to control myself. "What are the exact numbers?"
>
> The doctor glanced at the therapist, alarm engraved on his vast forehead. The other members of the group scowled at me: the woman who had shown us the scars from her cutting rites; the man who had recounted a graphic nightmare involving his mother and a boa constrictor; the woman who had given us a detailed account of her seduction of a married man. They were all appalled by my unseemly questions.
>
> "Carol, the issue here is feelings, not dollar signs," the therapist intoned. "Let's leave those details to the IRS."

Concern about money has been identified as the potential root of a host of personal problems including anxiety, depression, paranoia, impotence, impulse spending, gambling, social isolation, suicide, and murder. Yet there is something about money that has gagged us as well as the professional community of therapists. As the psychologist Trachtman writes, "It is perhaps the most ignored subject in the practice, literature and training of psychotherapy." Others in the field have pointed out the same void. Psychologist David Lansky described how during his fifteen years of clinical practice, financial issues rarely came up, because therapists don't bring them up. "They don't ask because they don't feel competent or culturally empowered to raise issues about money, about its meaning and impact on the lives of their clients," Lansky says. "It's a quandary then, isn't it? We know from common sense alone that concerns about money are ubiquitous in how we conduct our lives, and they have a central place in the problems that people in fact do bring to therapy . . . Yet, because of their unique set of blinders, therapists rarely hear the sound of money."

A handful of psychologists are building specialties in the financial psychology of money, and a larger group of financial planners are covering clients' personal relationships to money as a keystone of their practices. The problem is this: What little is being done by therapists and advisers concentrates on one's individual relationship with money, or the role of money in one's marriage or family. So those who are compulsive spenders, secret shoppers, money hoarders, or the like could, with some searching, find someone to help them unravel those issues in a therapeutic environment. Likewise, someone embroiled in family bickering over an estate plan, for example, could connect with a financial planner versed in psychological issues or working in tandem with such a therapist. Those fields and arrangements are relatively recent, but they exist for those knowledgeable and motivated enough to seek them out.

What is not being addressed—yet—is the social psychology of money. Social psychologists are not licensed as clinical practitioners and don't see patients. Psychologists and therapists who do take appointments still see our problems largely as our individual issues,

41

and the connection hasn't formally been made that we are all stewing in a societal soup of discontent. The context of our financial issues hasn't been broadened to examine us in the context of our friendships, neighborhood, cohort group, larger community, and culture. These exert a tremendous influence over our *perception* of our well-being, and therefore over our actual well-being. If we are not consciously taking into account and confronting these influences, they are building and bending our reality for us without our even realizing it. And while we let the cause remain out of our hands, so too will effective recovery remain elusive, even for those proactive enough to get themselves into therapy.

When Tina revealed the hidden credit card debt to her therapist, she was told she had to confess to her husband, to break the destructive cycle of shopping and secrecy. What she wasn't told was how common her problem is, which could have been a helpful context in which to begin confronting her personal issues with secret debt. In the "Secrets, Lies and Money" survey by *Money* magazine, nearly half the spouses surveyed said they have lied to their partners about what they've bought or how much they've paid for a purchase. Credit counselors routinely work with only half of a married couple on managing debt. "I can't tell you how many notes I've made that say, 'Don't leave message! Husband doesn't know,'" says Howard Dvorkin, who founded Consolidated Credit Counseling Services. Suze Orman, on her weekly personal finance show, says that questions about hidden credit card debt are very common. When the issue comes up, she recommends that spouses check each other's credit reports, as often as quarterly if a partner has had a spending problem. That's the length to which Orman thinks we must go to force honesty about money—and that's with the person you sleep next to at night.

Before Tina mustered the courage to reveal the credit card balance to her husband, he brought it up himself. He got home one night and found Tina in another new outfit. *What's that?* he asked her. His tone was different from usual. He was agitated. Before Tina could answer, he asked, *And what's going on with your credit card? How much have you charged on it?*

He knew she had been charging again because he had come across a bill several weeks before. He had tried to put it in the back of his mind while he focused on training for the marathon. Now, a week before the race, he couldn't hold off. He thought back to having paid off the balance once, to having cut up the card, and he felt taken advantage of.

Even though Tina had planned to tell John about the debt, she cringed at being exposed. This was the scene she had been dreading for months: the public accounting of her problem, her husband's anger. She started crying. John stood in front of her, unaffected.

How much is it? he asked.

Tina kept mumbling through her tears about it being worse than he thought.

How much? he asked her sternly.

Twenty.

John paused to grasp the mountain of debt that had grown behind his back.

Twenty exactly? he asked.

Twenty-one.

That was the worst of it for both of them, having the $21,000 secret dragged between them. But having the truth come out also allowed Tina to stop the spiral. She stopped shopping and taking refuge in nights out on the town. John decided they would pay off the debt by increasing their home equity line of credit, and he made Tina handle the application, something he knew she would dread. He made sure the credit card account was closed down this time.

A month later they found out she was pregnant. That gave her a mission in life and solved her immediate career dilemma.

There was one last mystery about the money next door that I wanted to unsheathe: What, during that whole period, had John and Tina been thinking about our side of the wall? Did they wonder what money we had or didn't have? Had they realized we were stressed? Had they ever compared, as we had, Tina going back to design school with my husband going back to business school? As a denouement, I asked them these questions and waited expectantly.

They looked back at me blankly. I could tell they weren't being coy or just polite.

"Well, you're homeowners," John said flatly, as if that explained everything. "You had your place before we moved in, so you probably didn't pay that much for it. You always seemed to have work. And your husband worked. And when he went back to school, you probably took out loans."

A tidy package of noninterest.

Tina added that they wonder more about what their friends think of them. "For the most part we have more than our friends, and we always feel weird about that and feel uncomfortable."

"I always feel we're a mystery to people," John said. "You weren't a mystery."

Ah, but we were, as we all are. Even though we thought we had them figured out, John and Tina were a mystery to us. And although they hadn't given much thought to us, we were a mystery to them too. While I had built John and Tina into our mythical Joneses, Tina had made her wealthy clients into her personal Joneses. And no doubt the client she most envied feels the tug to keep up with a particular someone in her circle. We all have them, the Joneses are always there—even though they don't actually exist.

John and Tina had a safety net: They had family money to support them when their spending slid out of control. Most Americans don't have that luxury. And when they try to keep up with the Joneses, it can turn disastrous—all behind closed doors.

CHAPTER THREE

⚬~

Keeping Up with the Joneses

At first they were fortunate. And they knew it.

Dan and Tammy grew up in working-class families in the South and were married shortly after high school. He started out at minimum wage on the ground floor of a retail chain store, she worked as a secretary. They lived rent-free with family to save money, then moved into an apartment of their own. Dan wondered, at times, why Tammy was so cautious with their money. Often when he suggested they go out to Olive Garden for dinner, she turned him down and instead went to the Publix grocery store. Her father had worked in manufacturing and her mother was a homemaker skilled at stretching a dollar. For many years, Tammy drove the car her parents had given her when she turned sixteen. Not until Dan and Tammy made the five years of payments on Dan's car did they invest in a new one for her. Their frugality paid off: In their midtwenties, when most of their friends weren't even married yet, they bought a quarter-acre lot of land and had a house built.

They waited several years before starting a family. Both were working hard, both got promotions, and children seemed like too huge a responsibility. Eventually, though, everything seemed to come together at once. Dan was promoted to a manager position, Tammy was pregnant, and when they were relocated for Dan's job, she stopped working to be a stay-at-home mom.

They lived in a rental close to the beach while having a three-bedroom house built nearby, in a fast-growing coastal community in southern Florida. They spent a pleasantly anguish-filled year deciding on the property, the house's floor plan, then the fixtures and the finishes. They expected to be settled in there for a long time. When it neared completion, Dan considered it the nicest house on the block.

The community was friendly and relaxed, home to many retirees and middle-income families. Among their closest friends—who, like them, were all married with young children—one husband worked as a sales rep for a flooring store, another was a technician at a hospital, and a third was an aviation mechanic. Dan and Tammy had met them all through the local play group. Tammy's days revolved around meeting the other mothers for story hours at the local public library or for play dates at their homes, where the living-room floors were covered with toys.

They hadn't even finished unpacking in their new house when Dan got a call from work: *You're being transferred.* He was being moved to Orlando, to manage a bigger store. The couple had to sell their brand-new house, at a loss, and relocate.

The Realtor in Orlando showed them several houses, but one suburban neighborhood in particular captivated them. It was a fifteen-year-old planned community on the outskirts of the city, still expanding within its gates. Driving in was like entering another world. One turn from a busy street and they were enveloped by a shady, tree-lined entryway. Inside, the lawns were groomed like golf courses, with mounds of impatiens, blooming hibiscus trees, and bushes carved like giant dinner rolls. There were man-made lakes, majestic fountains, bricked lanes, and a low speed limit enforced by speed bumps. On their first drive through, Dan kept thinking, *This is so nice!* Tammy loved that there were so many families with children. Dan liked the idea that it was so safe, that when he was working late in the evenings he would know that hoodlums couldn't reach their house. When the Realtor talked up the barbecues and kids' activities held at the club, Dan had visions of lounging around the pool with his wife and kids on the weekends he didn't have to work.

It would be somewhat of a reach, buying a house in that neighborhood. But they could afford it—something Tammy had to convince Dan of—even though they would have to pay about 15 percent more than what they had planned on paying. They won a bid on a new four-bedroom house, one more bedroom than they had been looking for. It seemed like a lot of money, a *lot* of money. But Dan's salary would cover it. They had been married for nearly a decade and were often told what great credit they had. They didn't have a car payment or other loans. They used credit cards, but they kept the balances low and would pay them off every time Dan got a bonus payment of a few thousand dollars. Dan had also just started to receive some stock options from his employer. If the company did well, these would become more valuable over time. Their financial situation was only improving. The mortgage would slowly shrink, while Dan got raises and larger bonuses and more options.

Or at least that's how it could have gone.

The Joneses were a crowd Dan and Tammy had hardly encountered before: professionals, entrepreneurs, highly educated people with ambition bordering on aggression. At first the young couple was proud of their new nest. But suddenly, rather than having one of the nicest houses in the neighborhood, they were living on the low end. Surrounding them were people they looked up to, who had done better, gotten farther, had more. The couple they became best friends with owned their own business and lived in a house worth triple the value of Dan and Tammy's. Another friend sold his company and became a multimillionaire almost overnight. Tammy eventually became close with the wife of a pro sports player.

Dan and Tammy met many of these friends, as they had their old ones, through the local Mommy & Me group. But this group was different from the one in the old neighborhood. Instead of going to the library, they took morning day trips to Disney World, the Science Center or Universal Studios, where the families all had passes. Dan and Tammy bought passes too. When the mothers did meet in their homes, Tammy stepped into enormous properties, with inground pools and four-car garages. To maintain them and still have free time, the women hired an array of services: professional cleaners, gardeners, and nannies. Tammy painted the inside of their house herself, and she and Dan did their own yard work; but after a while she agreed with her friends that a housecleaner, at least, was worth the extra expense.

Their new friends seemed especially anxious about their children's development. They sent them to lessons and camps of all sorts, and they talked, even over diapers, of preparation for college. When Dan and Tammy were growing up, she joined sports teams through public school and a youth group through church, and he explored the local woods and canoed and fished with his brother. Now they learned about toys that tutored, birthday parties with petting zoos, and tennis camp for kindergartners that cost $200 per week. Within a year or so of moving to Orlando, they gave in to the peer pressure to join the local country club. At first they invested in a basic-level membership that had the lowest monthly fee and a two-figure monthly minimum on dining service. After their second child was born, they upgraded the membership to one that included the racquet courts and pool. Tammy followed her friends into the ladies' tennis league, a circle that required not only court fees and extensive coaching, but skirted white outfits and hours of child care.

Away from the club, a main social activity of Tammy's became shopping with her friends. They spent many afternoons at the mall constructing and reconstructing various wardrobes. Tammy upgraded her clothing, and she outfitted her children in many matching ensembles. At the checkout, she took advantage of the discount given to her when she opened credit accounts. As she returned to the circuit of stores and used the cards, the credit limits grew.

Their social life in the evenings was also transformed. Friends invited Dan and Tammy out to expensive restaurants. The crowd dressed stylishly and ordered bottles of vintage wine from the bottom of the list. To these couples, it was routine to spend on dinner what at first seemed to Dan and Tammy to be a small fortune. But they came to think, *This must be how people live.*

It wasn't how most people live.

When Dan and Tammy moved into their first apartment, they were making a household income within a few hundred dollars of the national median. So half of everyone else in the country was doing better than they were, and the other half not as well. When they built their first home two years later, they were ahead of most people their age: Only 38 percent of households headed by someone under age 35 owned their home.

The city they moved to in southern Florida, where they started their family, fell into the lower half of the country in terms of prosperity, measured by the income of its residents and home values. Within the town, Dan and Tammy firmly belonged to the upper echelon. Even with Tammy not working, their family brought in about twice the amount of money as those around them. Neither Dan nor Tammy had a college degree, but that didn't set them apart from the vast majority of their neighbors: Only 1 in 6 people in town had graduated from college. (Nationwide, the figure is 1 in 4.) In that environment, they were prospering.

Then came the call to relocate to Orlando. And the decision to move behind the gates.

The community inside the gates looked like a different world to Dan and Tammy, and it was. Dan felt proud that they had really moved up socially. In reality, relative to those around them, their status plummeted.

Most of the people living in their new neighborhood had graduated from college. Income-wise, Dan had far outpaced his peers nationwide who only had high school diplomas. By that time, he was making more money than most people in the country with a master's degree. But he was not, by a long shot, making more money than most of his neighbors. Families in the midrange of this community made more than double the national median income, and the median home was more than twice as expensive. Dan and Tammy fell into the lower half of the community's pay scale. And the house they bought, although expensive to them, was one of the cheapest inside the gates.

The year after Dan and Tammy moved into the new neighborhood, they bought a used SUV. Instead of financing it with an auto loan, they decided to pay for it by using the home equity line of credit that had been offered to them automatically when they signed their mortgage. Why not take advantage of the lower interest rate and the tax deductibility of the interest, they reasoned; then they would just pay it down like they would have paid an auto loan. They ended up not making as large a monthly payment as they would have on a term loan, however, so the car wasn't getting paid off as quickly.

They had always managed to save, but now, for life inside the gates, they started using all of their income. And a little more. Tammy had her hair colored every few weeks. She joined a top health club. It cost a premium over what a more basic gym charged, but she justified it because of how much better their child care was. The kids had a spacious playroom, and the staff kept them occupied with lots of games. Tammy could work out for two hours and take time to shower without ever worrying about them. After her workout, they would often have lunch together at the club's cafe, which was expensive but convenient.

Tammy's friends went one after another to the plastic surgeon for breast implants. Tammy, too, got the $5,000 operation, charged to a credit card.

Dan took up gourmet cooking, hunting down esoteric ingredients that would be used only for a single special recipe. On the weekends, they started accepting invitations to couples getaways to the beach. Instead of going for the day, they checked into oceanfront hotels for one or two nights. Once going on beach vacations became usual, they ventured farther away for annual vacations together. Following tips from their friends and sometimes traveling with them, they scheduled ski trips out West and stayed at trendy resorts. Then they took a different vacation every year with the kids.

No matter how much larger they lived, though, the people around them seemed to have more, be doing more, and generally enjoying a more exciting life. Their houses were more spacious, their cars more impressive, their parties always catered, their furniture made out of unheard-of species of woods. And these people were constantly traveling: to Las Vegas, to the Bahamas, to Latin America, to Europe. Dan and Tammy didn't see themselves as any different, and they felt they deserved the same as everyone else. *They're no smarter than I am*, Dan thought. *Their work ethic is no better than mine.* So why was everyone else's life more cushioned? Making matters worse was that the friends they met when they first moved in were all moving up, upgrading their lifestyles much more quickly than Dan and Tammy could keep pace. Tammy started to feel anxious about their life: Was she dressing well enough? Did the kids feel inferior when they went over to play at nicer houses? Shouldn't they themselves move into a larger house? Why wasn't Dan more ambitious?

For the first time in years, money got tight. More money than ever before was coming in, but even more was flowing out. Dan started getting larger bonuses, well into five figures. However, the amounts were unpredictable. Tammy, who had handled the household finances since the day they were married, let the balances on the credit cards creep up, always intending to pay everything off with the coming bonus. But once the bonus arrived, it wasn't enough. She asked Dan to cash in some of the stock options. That would make up for the shortfall. Her husband agreed and didn't ask questions.

To conserve the money coming in, Tammy started making minimum payments on the credit card accounts. The balances grew and multiplied. The more of their credit lines they used, the higher their interest rates were raised, from what had been a usual single-digit figure to as high as nearly 25 percent. That pushed the balances up higher and made even the minimum payments more expensive.

They didn't rein in their expenditures. They had a lot of money coming in, a lot of resources to fall back on, so Tammy didn't worry. It was just a matter of managing the cash flow, she thought. Dan consistently got raises, and there always seemed to be a bonus on the horizon. If things were tight, it was only temporary, she assured herself. In the meantime, the home equity line of credit, which had an interest rate now significantly lower than that of the cards, could easily be raised. With a phone call to the bank and a visit to sign the documents, they had several thousand more dollars at their disposal. When the checking account ran short, it was easy to transfer $1,000 or $2,000 from the equity line to the checking account just by tapping out the instruction at the ATM.

They still owned a lot of options, too, which was another easy way to flood the household accounts with cash, temporarily. Once they sold some the first time, they saw how easy it was to make a phone call and receive a check in the mail. Then their account balances ran high for a while, and they could shop or go out without worrying about not being able to afford it. They took on home improvement projects—putting in granite countertops and new appliances, replacing the light fixtures, taking up the carpet and replacing it with hardwood floors—that made their home look more like everyone else's around them. And they were continually in the market for the perfect sofa. *My husband has a good job*, Tammy told herself. *He gets stock and bonuses. We can afford it.*

Except one year the bonus was significantly smaller than what they had quickly grown used to. They needed it to pay down the debts that had accumulated, but it wouldn't cover a fraction of them. They needed money to keep up with their monthly expenses, so Tammy didn't put the bonus toward the balances on credit cards or the equity line and instead put the money toward financing their lifestyle. When they ran through the bonus money, she asked Dan to cash more options. A couple of months later, she had to ask again. Then again.

That's when Dan realized something was wrong. And getting worse. He knew they had been living large, and that they hadn't been able to rely on his regular paycheck income for some time. But since Tammy handled the money, he didn't know the details of how the credit balances had grown. *We should slow down*, he told his wife when she asked him to cash more options. She recoiled. *We can afford it*, she insisted. *You're about to get your bonus.*

She was right, the annual bonus was coming. And it was huge. By far the largest bonus they had ever gotten, it totaled nearly $100,000—much more than Dan's annual salary. Whatever problems they had gotten themselves into financially, this was going to resolve them. They would pay everything off and start over with a clean slate, the way they always used to.

Dan needed to make sure of it, though. Subconsciously he had known they were getting into trouble—otherwise they wouldn't have needed to supplement his income with stock sales—but he had trusted that Tammy was keeping everything under control. Now, with a Big Fix around the corner, he was ready to face up to the problem because he knew he could solve it. For the first time, Dan told his wife to give him all of their account statements. One night after work, he retreated with them into their home office.

He had never handled their personal finances before, and now he realized he needed to be methodical to get the detailed picture. Using the Internet, he figured out how to order a copy of each of their credit reports. He printed them out, not paying much attention to the card balances they listed because he knew those could be a couple of months out of date. What he used the credit reports for was to make sure he knew about each of their open accounts. Then he started going down the list. Using the stack of statements, he wrote down the current balance for each card. For the accounts he didn't have statements for, he called the companies for the up-to-date balances. Then he got out the calculator. As a store manager he was used to tallying up figures, but when he hit the total key he saw at a glance that he had been careless and made an entry error.

He started down the list again: American Express, MasterCard, Visa, another Visa, another MasterCard, Discover, Gap, Dillard's, Macy's, Ann Taylor . . . Again he hit the total key. This time he stared at it in disbelief. It showed the same figure he had seen a couple of minutes before. The one he had been certain was a mistake. A panicky feeling came over him. He felt sick. Overwhelmed. He had been deceived—not necessarily by his wife, but by himself—and uncovering the deception felt almost like finding out his spouse had had an affair. She hadn't shared with him how they had been falling farther and farther behind, and he had been looking the other way for too long. On credit cards alone, the couple owed nearly $100,000.

Tammy maps the slippery slope back to being given the home equity line of credit with their mortgage, and then using it. Dan traces their trouble to associating with people of higher means and attempting to match their lifestyle. The combination of having credit available and dipping into it to satisfy desires is a cocktail most of us have tasted. Living beyond our means is a habit easy to renounce yet difficult to resist.

Tapping home equity as a source of credit is a common tool that can become a financial death trap. Home equity becomes available to borrow against when a home is worth a certain amount more than the mortgage owed on it. That can happen by paying down the mortgage or—especially common in recent years with the real estate boom—the home's value rising with the market. A homeowner can take a home equity loan, which means borrowing a fixed amount of money to be paid back over a set number of years in monthly installments, which is why it is referred to as a second mortgage. An owner can also open a home equity line of credit, which is a pre-approved loan that doesn't have to be used at all, or it can be used all at once or in bites as needed, then paid back and reborrowed on a continual basis up to the credit limit, like a big credit card. The interest rates on home equity debt are lower than is typical on credit cards, and the interest is tax deductible within certain limits. Banks are usually quick to approve these loans backed by real estate.

The danger is that, unlike with credit card debt, which is unsecured, if borrowers have trouble making payments on home equity debt, they can lose their homes. So the arrangement is relatively low risk to the lender but relatively high risk to the borrower. "Lenders have continued to promote this product aggressively by waiving closing costs and other fees, offering low introductory interest rates, and increasing the acceptable limits on loan-to-value ratios," states a report by the Federal Reserve.

Historically, according to surveys by the Federal Reserve, home equity is borrowed against to pay for home improvements and to repay other debts. At the time Dan and Tammy were closing on their house in Orlando, the Fed reported a new development in home equity borrowing: "Credit lines were found to have additional uses not often found for most traditional loans, including vehicle purchases, education, and vacations." As Dan and Tammy were using their home equity line to pay for a car, 37 percent of borrowers used home equity lines for the same purpose. A third used their credit lines to borrow, for whatever purpose, as much money as Dan and Tammy did: $25,000 or more. Dan and Tammy and those around them in the gated community were typical customers for home equity borrowing. Most people with a home equity line had incomes above $50,000 per year, and a third were making at least $75,000.

As Dan and Tammy grew up and started their own family, the personal finances of the country as a whole were shifting negatively. More Americans bought houses, but on average they ended up owning less of their homes due to the rise in home equity borrowing. During the same time period, we stopped saving as much and started loading up on credit card debt. In 1981 families saved an average of 11 percent of their income and owed 4 percent of their income on credit cards. By 2000 the average savings had fallen below zero, which means we've gone into debt to spend more than we make. Credit card debt had risen to 12 percent of income.

The credit card industry mushroomed in the 1990s. Between 1993 and 2000, the countrywide credit card limit grew from $777 billion to $3 trillion. Only counting Visas and MasterCards, American households carry an average of five of these cards. How much do we owe on our credit cards? That's hard to say. Apparently a lot of us either don't know our balances or don't want to disclose them, even anonymously. When the Federal Reserve surveys consumers, the self-reported results show an average household balance on credit cards of $4,126. But when that figure is compared to how much the lending industry says we have borrowed from it on cards, the figure is about three times higher, at around $12,000. When we report our attitudes about the use of credit cards there is also a discrepancy between what we say and how much trouble, on the whole, we are in. A Federal Reserve report states, "Cardholders' opinions about their own experiences are almost the reverse of their views about consumers' experiences in general, suggesting considerable concern over the behavior of others and possibly a belief that 'I can handle credit cards, but other people cannot.'"

Lending practices have gotten more lenient, with more people being offered more and more credit, while terms of borrowing have gotten more onerous. So credit is easier to get but harder to manage. Grace periods during which a balance can be repaid without owing any interest, or a payment can be late without penalty, have been shortened or eliminated. Fees have jumped. And while introductory interest rate offers abound, they are canceled and often raised past 20 percent if a payment is late. Regular interest rates, too, are being raised for a greater variety of reasons, such as a card company deeming balances too high, or finding out a utility bill has been paid late. And while the interest charges have gone up with the higher rates, the minimum amount that must be repaid every month on the balance has gone down, from an old norm of 5 percent to about half that now. So customers paying the minimums take longer to pay off balances. If Dan and Tammy were to keep making minimum payments on their cards—which were costing them more than half of their take-home pay—it would take over fifty years to pay them off.

From the time he learned about their debts, Dan took over his family's finances. He put the big bonus toward their credit card accounts, despite the protests of Tammy, who thought the money needed to be saved. After taxes were taken out, the lump sum covered about 60 percent of the debt.

When he opened the card statements every month, though, he saw their spending hadn't slowed. Tammy would charge $2,000 or more in a month on a single store card for clothes. Dan surreptitiously made upgrades to his car, putting the charges on cards. They both lost the fear of debt that they had held for so long. Once they started relying on credit to support their lifestyle, it was difficult to stop. Nor did they acknowledge to themselves that they really did have to stop. They both relied on another big bonus coming, on selling stock options to cover the income gap.

Their debt was snowballing. With high interest rates and since they were still adding charges, the balances grew faster than they could be paid down. Some months it was hard to pay bills and make all of the minimum payments. They dipped into the home equity line of credit. When that was used up, they sometimes had to charge a utility bill. The "convenience checks" that periodically came in the mail from the credit card companies started being used to pay off other card accounts. When cash ran out before a payday, they took cash advances.

Dan didn't understand how anyone making such a decent income could be in such a disastrous financial situation. He talked with his wife about lowering their expenses, giving up some luxuries. Like the country club membership, he said. They were paying several hundred dollars every month so that she could play tennis and lunch with friends and the kids could go swimming. They could do without it, he argued. They *had* to do without it. *If we had a pool in our backyard*, she negotiated, *then we could cancel the membership.*

He worked out the math, comparing how much the monthly

payments would be on taking an additional loan from the home equity line of credit to pay for a pool, versus how much they were spending on the club membership. Seeing that it would indeed lower their monthly expenses, he agreed to the bargain. They applied for yet another increase in the home equity line and converted the whole credit line to a second mortgage that was nearly equal to the amount of their first mortgage. That paid for the pool to be put in. The only thing was, they never canceled the club membership.

Nor did they stop going out, both together and, increasingly, alone. For the first dozen years of their marriage it had been rare for either of them ever to go out in the evening without the other one. But slowly, at first imperceptibly, their interests diverged. Going out became increasingly important to Tammy—going out to the fashionable places, wearing the right outfit, making sure they were keeping up with the right crowd. When they went out to dinner, they moved on afterward with everyone else to a bar or a club. They stayed out until early morning before coming home to pay the babysitter for a six- or seven-hour shift. Tammy still found it fun and relaxing, while Dan started to find it stressful and exhausting. Some evenings he stayed home with the kids while his wife went out with friends.

How can she keep spending? Dan wondered, as he looked at account statements with charges for thousands of dollars. Later he would ask the same question about himself. What had *he* been thinking? Why couldn't he stand his ground, why didn't he insist on controlling themselves? The only answer he could come up with was that he was trying his hardest to keep his family happy. Being able to spend money, to shop and to go out with friends and to live the way they did, was the only thing that seemed to make his wife content anymore. He held hope that, by using the stock options and by receiving big bonuses, they would somehow be able to keep up. He dreaded saying no to her, disappointing her, seeing her miserable, causing arguments—especially if the children might overhear.

When they did argue, often when Dan had just opened a credit card statement and confronted her about it, Tammy had started to blame him outright, saying that their problem was that he didn't earn enough money. Why did the husbands among their friends do so much better? Dan couldn't figure out—yet he didn't try that hard to think it through—how they had gone so wrong, how they used to be happy on so little; and how now, with his earning several times what he used to when they were younger, he couldn't satisfy her.

The cash flow got tighter and tighter. Card accounts were hitting their ceilings. A couple of times cards were rejected at the cash register for being over their limits. They went to a furniture store and picked out a new bedroom set, which they tried to put on store credit. A few minutes after filling out the application, the saleswoman came back to them and said she was sorry, that the application had been denied. *No big deal*, Tammy said. *What?!* Dan asked. He told the saleswoman that they must have made a mistake. *Let me see the application*, he said, *you must have written down our Social Security numbers wrong*. He checked them, but they were correct. *Fine*, he said, handing over a credit card, *we'll pay for half of it now*. The charge went through, but later, at home, Dan knew that they didn't have any way to pay the other half of the bill and take delivery of the furniture. He called the store to cancel the order. A letter arrived in the mail explaining that their application for store credit had been denied because of their high credit balances. Dan was still in shock that they had been turned down, after so many years of stellar credit. He couldn't believe that they had hit some kind of limit.

Then one night he did believe it. He sat in his office to juggle the bills and figure out how to keep everything paid up, to get by until the next check. As he went over their accounts, he realized that they had maxed out everything. Except for a few store accounts, there was no credit left. There was no more going to the home equity line of credit, since the house was fully leveraged. All of the cards were at their limits. There wasn't any money at all in their checking account. He didn't know how he was going to pay for gas to get to work and make it through to payday. Then he remembered one limited resource: They kept two cans of fuel in the garage for the lawn mower. He would use that for his commute.

Dan kept a close watch on the cards. If he paid $500 for a minimum payment and that freed up $100 of their credit line, he knew he could spend $100. If he didn't know off the top of his head which cards had a scrap of credit available, he would go online and look them up before they went out, to save the embarrassment of having a card declined in front of friends.

To his relief, they made it through to bonus time again. The payout was a fraction of the previous year's bonanza, but he was determined to make this one last. It would make up for the monthly shortfall and see them through the rest of the year. They could make their minimum payments and then some. It would last, he promised. This time, it really would last.

Except it didn't. It was like dropping a single planeful of water onto a forest in flames. The money evaporated within two months.

As Tammy had done, Dan turned to cashing stock options. With the extra liquidity, they could continue overspending. To celebrate their anniversary, they booked an extravagant vacation. There wasn't room to charge on any of the credit cards, so they withdrew cash they had gotten from selling stock. As they were checking out of an expensive resort, Dan watched two other couples who were traveling together checking in. After one of the men handed over his credit card, the desk clerk, attempting to preapprove charges on the card, told him that the card hadn't gone through. Dan watched the drama unfold. He saw panic in the guy's face and almost saw sweat start to bead on his forehead. The man didn't come up with another card. Instead, he leaned over the counter and said to the hotel clerk in a low voice, *See if you can put $720 on it.*

Dan understood exactly what was going on. The man had miscalculated how much credit was available on the card, and Dan could relate to it. The couple was as strapped as Dan and Tammy were, and yet they were both on vacation at a luxury resort. The man had to turn to his friend, who was standing at the other end of the counter, and tell him there was some problem with his card and ask if he minded putting their room on his friend's card. The friend looked confused, Dan thought, probably wondering why he was paying for the other guy's room, but he reluctantly handed over his card. *We'll settle up when we get back*, the guy with the maxed-out card said, acting as if it were no big deal. As if there were a lot of money back home, Dan commented to himself. He knew the situation so well. They were both going to return home to financial ruins.

The vacation would be the last possible break from reality. Dan started cashing options every few weeks to keep up with the bills, the mortgage, the second mortgage, the credit card payments, and their other expenses. The money was soaked up almost as quickly as it came in. When he got preapproved credit card offers in the mail, he called to accept them. As he was turned down by each one, he started to realize there really was going to be an end.

Dan and Tammy both knew the situation was grave, but they kept kidding themselves that more money coming in would fix it. They didn't talk about it. Dan still dreaded disappointing his wife by insisting that they could not, they clearly could *not*, live the lifestyle they had adopted. They had lived far beyond their means for more than three years, and even if they cut back at that point, the debt had already taken on a life of its own. They had been living on safety nets—the equity line, the options, the unpredictable bonuses—

and were finally falling through. Dan's regular income barely covered their first and second mortgage payments and the minimum payments on their nearly twenty credit cards. There was never any money in the checking account. Paychecks came in and went out immediately. So did the large checks from selling stock. They had already seen the Big Fix bonus happen once, and even that hadn't saved them.

Late one night, Dan sat alone in his home office. He had just cashed the very last stock options that they owned, for a take-home of a little more than $3,000. It wasn't even going to make a dent in what was owed that very month. They had been putting groceries and gas on credit cards, but they couldn't beat back the balances quickly enough to continue to do that. The bank wasn't going to let them borrow any more against their home. Dan didn't think the store had done well enough that year for him to earn much of a bonus, and if he got any at all, the payment wouldn't arrive for over six months. There was no more going to the well. They were heading for default.

Their life as they had somehow managed to keep it going for several years was over. Dan told himself that his family life as he knew it was about to change. His mind racing, he had visions of their becoming homeless. *What am I going to do?* he kept asking himself, sitting at his desk in tears. And he prayed for help.

There are two kinds of games we play with our image. The first is what psychologists call "impression management," which is when you fool other people about who you are or what's going on with you. The second is "self-deception," which is less of a game and more of a subconscious strategy. That's when you honestly fool yourself.

Dan and Tammy suffered from both. On the impression management side, they tried to look as if they fit in where they didn't really belong. On the self-deception side, a problem was growing, but they didn't admit it to themselves. I kept searching in their story for rational behavior, for confrontations with reality. I kept asking versions of the same unanswered question: How could you do this to yourself? Why didn't you make changes? But it wasn't like that, Dan tried to explain. They really didn't see the problem for what it was. There was concern, he said, but not enough to motivate them to alter their lifestyle. "We didn't see it coming until close to the end," he said. "It absolutely sneaks up on you. It's amazing how much of a dire situation you can be in and not change it."

Amazing, but real. Denial is a common phenomenon for people sinking deeper into the muck of debt. Thinking things are not that bad, or that they will surely get better very soon, is a common affliction for people in a financial crisis, and it makes matters worse. Everyone thinks that they are different, that meltdown can't and won't happen to them. "I see a lot of ostrich behavior," says Glenn, a bankruptcy attorney. "The husband brings home the check and the wife handles the finances." Just like Dan and Tammy. "The husband thinks, 'We must be okay.'" Or they keep spending today with a plan to pay shortly thereafter. When the paycheck arrives. When the bonus comes. "When the money comes in," Glenn says, "nobody wants to use that money to pay off balances. They want to spend it on something fun. That's truly the culture of America." When you're in the cycle, it seems okay to go on that way, even though keeping up means falling further behind.

People who owe a lot of money are often unsure how much it is that they owe. Credit counselors describe couples hiding debt not only from each other but from themselves, in the form of not looking at statements and not adding up the total. Even in the midst of financial catastrophe, when they have gotten themselves to a credit counselor or a bankruptcy court, many people, Dan and Tammy included, are eager to describe how they've always had such great credit.

The night Dan realized they were facing the end, he turned to the Internet and started researching what was out there to help people mired in debt. He hated admitting to himself that they had gotten themselves into a situation they couldn't get out of, that he couldn't get them out of. But he was also staring down a precipice. Unless they got help somehow, it was about to get worse. His whole life he had never been more than a month late with a payment, but now he didn't have any more resources to keep paying the bills, which far outpaced his income. Almost immediately they would fall behind. Then they would start getting the dreaded collection calls from creditors. Dan didn't know how they would be able to stop the downward spiral.

The first possibility he looked into was debt consolidation. He found organizations online that promised to help people cope with uncontrollable amounts of debt. Some trumpeted that they could reduce the amount clients owed. Dan read their claims and dismissed most of the organizations as shams. One national organization seemed legitimate. Dan called them and made an appointment. He took his statements with him, sat down in an office across from a credit counselor, and explained the situation. He never had to get out his statements. Sitting behind a fishbowl of cut-up credit cards, the counselor told Dan that they couldn't help him. Dan hadn't yet fallen behind, the counselor pointed out. No late fees had piled up. It looked to creditors as if he were still perfectly able to pay his bills, so this organization wouldn't have any bargaining power with them. The counselor gave him a budgeting worksheet. *This might help you figure out where you can reduce your expenses*, he advised. But Dan knew that trimming was no longer going to help. They were too far gone.

He searched more online, looking for another solution. As he searched the keywords "debt" and "help," one thing kept coming up: bankruptcy. He had been avoiding even looking into it. *We couldn't possibly have to go bankrupt*, he thought. Surely the problem was not *that* severe. Filing for bankruptcy would be so shameful. It would mean he was the ultimate failure.

Who had he heard of declaring bankruptcy? Famous people who had frittered away millions of dollars. Corrupt corporations. Nobody like them, certainly. Nobody that they would know. And for good reason, he thought. Honest people, middle-class families like theirs, people with means, had no excuse for not being able to pay their bills. Whenever he had seen people on TV blaming creditors for their problems, he had thought, *That's ridiculous!* He had always had disdain for people who declared bankruptcy. Once a customer at his store had run up several thousand dollars on credit and later declared bankruptcy. Dan had had to write it off the store's books, and it had disgusted him. He had seen the customer as taking advantage, as taking the easy way out. He didn't want to see himself like that.

Much as he hated going to his wife with the problem that they so steadfastly avoided, she was the only person he could turn to. He eased into it, mentioning that he was researching the options, one of which was bankruptcy. Tammy dismissed it. *That can't happen*, she told him. *Just do something! Keep researching. There must be something else that will help us.*

He got a book on bankruptcy from the bookstore and checked out another one from the library. He tried to show some sections of the books to his wife, but she didn't want to talk about it. *I don't want to deal with this*, she told him. *You handle it.*

Dan went by himself to meet with a bankruptcy lawyer. Like most people who end up in Glenn's office, Dan couldn't believe he was there. He asked the lawyer for some kind of reassurance: *Does this happen to anyone like me? Does anybody else who makes as much money as I do ever have to file for bankruptcy?*

As Dan learned before he met with the attorney, there are two kinds of bankruptcy for most people. The first, and by far the most common, option is filing under Chapter 7 of the federal bankruptcy code, which is often referred to as a "liquidation" or "straight" bankruptcy.

The process is fairly straightforward: You file forms with the court listing your income and expenses, anything of value that you own, recent transactions, and all of your debts. A bankruptcy trustee appointed to the case is responsible for selling your "nonexempt" assets and using the proceeds to pay off your creditors to the extent possible. Nonexempt assets are anything beyond what the law allows you to protect for basic living and working, so you can generally keep your clothing (not furs, though) and personal property including some jewelry, investments in most retirement plans, the cash value of insurance policies, and in some states a vehicle with a certain amount of equity in it. Florida is one of the states in which you don't have to sell your home to pay creditors as long as you can keep paying the mortgage.

About a month after filing, a debtor has to come to a "meeting of creditors" at the courthouse. The trustee asks basic questions about assets and so forth, and if any creditors want to come and ask the debtor questions, they can do so at this meeting. In practice, it's rare for any creditors to show up. In most cases, the trustee doesn't end up discovering assets to liquidate either. Therefore the meeting of creditors takes a minute or two, after which the debts owed are discharged by the court. Some debts are not eligible to be forgiven, such as child support or alimony payments, certain taxes, student loans, and criminal fines. Secured debts, like mortgages or car payments, need to be reaffirmed if the debtor wants to keep the collateral. A reaffirmation agreement signed by the debtor means that the debt remains owed after the bankruptcy.

In Orlando's bankruptcy court meeting room for Chapter 7 filers, a trustee sat behind a desk with a computer and tape recorder on it, a flag standing in the corner, and a small Department of Justice medallion on the wall. The rest of the small room was crammed with rows of chairs, where debtors and sometimes their attorneys waited to be called. After the routine list of questions and usually yes or no answers, an exchange that was typical went like this:

TRUSTEE: "Good luck to you."

DEBTOR: "What do I do now?"

"Go home and wait for a discharge" [a letter stating that the debts are officially gone].

"This is it?"

"Yes, this is it."

From the procedural standpoint, it does look easy. And if you get into trouble again, you can declare bankruptcy again after eight years. I've attended meetings of creditors at the bankruptcy courts in New York and Florida and, to be frank, both times had the same reaction: *This is bullcrap.* That's how a lot of laypersons view the bankruptcy system: *Why are some people let off so easy, while the rest of us are honest and keep struggling?*

There are a couple of things to point out. The first is that most people who go bankrupt are not doing it because they want to get away with something. According to the Consumer Bankruptcy Project, an ongoing research project conducted by several universities, the majority of people going bankrupt do so as a result of losing their jobs, getting divorced, or incurring medical bills.

That said, yes, some people can take advantage. They are probably not owning up to having an ability to pay some debts, and might not feel any guilt about having their debts wiped clean by court order. But that can't be a significant percentage of the people who seek the relief of the bankruptcy system, a claim that has been supported by research at the American Bankruptcy Institute. As with anything, the system has to not work sometimes in order to work most of the time for the people who truly need it. Where is the line in terms of what constitutes taking advantage of the system? Glenn, who has a reputation as one of the top consumer bankruptcy attorneys in the Orlando area, defines abusers as "people who have knowledge of the system before they file, and manipulate circumstances beforehand. People who say, 'I'm going to run up my credit cards and then file bankruptcy.' A few years ago, you could get away with that. Not now."

Glenn explains the difference as a civil enforcement initiative put in place by the U.S. Trustees office in 2001 to clamp down on bankruptcy abuse. The initiative called for local trustees to review every bankruptcy petition with renewed vigor, scrutinize the availability of assets and the reasonability of the expenses claimed, and, if they saw anything fishy, to file a motion indicating a bad faith filing. If trustees see any way a filer can afford to repay some of his or her debts, they'll argue that the debtor can't seek Chapter 7 and can only pursue a Chapter 13 bankruptcy with a repayment plan. In Dan and Tammy's case, if it weren't for their self-inflated lifestyle and consequently debilitating credit card payments, Dan was making more than enough money for the family to live on. Under those circumstances, filing a Chapter 7 case and asking for the credit card debts to be discharged might have triggered a claim of bad faith. Consequently, Dan and Tammy went into Chapter 13 bankruptcy.

The other point to make about the apparent ease of filing for bankruptcy is that the legal process of discharging debts is separate from the emotional turmoil that most debtors suffer, first from being in so much debt, and then from deciding to resort to bankruptcy. What the average observer sees in bankruptcy court is a slice of the formal part of the process; it doesn't reveal the meat of the action, what going bankrupt means in the personal lives of the debtors.

The second kind of bankruptcy, Chapter 13, is a little more involved. It is often called "reorganization bankruptcy" or a "wage-earner's plan." In this scenario, the debtor can't afford full payment of debts but can pay something. Unlike in Chapter 7, no property is sold to pay creditors (although, as in Chapter 7, if you fall behind on your mortgage payments, the house can still be foreclosed on). Instead, the debtor can take a certain allowance to live on, and the rest of his or her earnings is turned over every month to a bankruptcy trustee, who pays creditors according to a plan approved by the court. This goes on for three to five years, after which most remaining debts are discharged by the court. Debts that cannot be discharged under Chapter 13 include child support or alimony debts, certain taxes, student loans, and ongoing mortgage payments.

Bankruptcy reforms approved by Congress in the spring of 2005 that went into effect that October make it more difficult to file any bankruptcy, and they put stricter limits on who can go into Chapter 7 bankruptcy. The new rules compare debtors' incomes to the state median, applying additional standards for those earning above the median amount. Another major change is that instead of letting a judge decide if a debtor's living expenses are reasonable, the court calculates how much a debtor is allowed to live on based on IRS guidelines for family size and geographic location. A law firm in California explains the new law on its Web site like this: "The presumption that a debtor is entitled to relief from his debts is effectively replaced by presumptions that the debtor's filing is abusive until the debtor proves otherwise."

Glenn's office, in a high-rise building in downtown Orlando, very much resembles a doctor's office, with a receptionist sitting behind a sliding-glass window, shelves stuffed with tabbed manila folders, and end tables in the waiting room stacked with issues of magazines like *People* and *Baby Talk*, well-thumbed but probably unread. When a client comes in, Glenn always starts by asking them how they're doing, and many respond with some version of *Well, I'm not good, because I'm here.* The first appointment is usually punctuated by a lot of tears, admissions of shame, and anger—at themselves and at each other, if a husband and wife have come in together. A lot of people want to size themselves up even among the bankrupt population and want to know the same thing Dan did: *Am I the only one in this situation?* They say to Glenn, *Please say you've seen worse than this.*

The truth is that Glenn is seeing "worse" cases all the time. By "worse" he means people of higher and higher incomes, people one wouldn't expect to be overburdened by debts. When he started practicing bankruptcy law nearly a decade ago, the average client was a minority earning $8 or $9 an hour. Now more clients are in the middle class, earning $38,000, $60,000, even over $100,000. Some have lost jobs, some have been hit by medical expenses, but some are also like Dan and Tammy, caught in a whirlwind of living beyond their means.

"When I was a kid," Glenn says of growing up in the late 1960s and early '70s, "the BMWs and Mercedeses were driven by the doctors and the lawyers, not twenty-three-year-olds just out of college. There's been a societal shift to style over substance. And the amount and pervasiveness of advertising has increased. There are constant messages: *You need this. You need this. You need this. You need this.*"

Glenn's wife is also an attorney, in a different field. They don't see eye-to-eye on the use of credit. When she suggested using a home equity line of credit to pay for an extension on their house—after all, she said, she was about to get a distribution from her firm—Glenn said, *No way.* For him to be comfortable, first the money has to be in hand, then spent, and never the other way around. He carries one credit card, for use in case of an emergency. "I go home and see my wife use a credit card and I panic," he says. The people he sees in his office on a daily basis are too much like Glenn and his wife for him to feel safe from the slippery slope of indebtedness. He sees so clearly how it can happen, and how it does happen. "I go home and see twelve preapproved loans in the mail with pictures of homes and cruises, and part of me says, *I must be doing really well. These are the banks, they must know!* But then I know they are marketing gimmicks, because every day I see people in my office crying because they took advantage of these offers. I see it for what it is, but they don't. There has to be responsibility taken by the creditors. I think there really is this pusher out there."

From Glenn's perspective, most people taking on debt don't see the crisis building until it's too late. The balances rise, the interest rates are raised, the minimum payments get harder to pay, just as it happened with Dan and Tammy. They keep juggling and not really adding things up until, like Dan, they suddenly see a month when there is no way to pay. And there's not going to be any way to pay. Then they surface in Glenn's office, past the breaking point.

The hardest moment for Dan was realizing that they were actually going to go through with bankruptcy. *How could this have happened?* he wondered. How had he failed as a provider? Part of him wondered if his wife hadn't been right, if he couldn't have thrown himself into work more, worked longer hours, and been more aggressive about promotions.

Dan hadn't gone to college, but he had still made something of himself. He had built a successful career and made what he assured himself was more money than most people made who only had a high school education and started out at an hourly wage. He had two great children, and he constantly prayed that he would be as much of a role model for them as his father had been for him. Dan adored his father and his upbringing in a family of very modest means that had still provided him a wonderful childhood. Dan and his wife had started out so very happy, at a time when they had little money and few opportunities to travel or go out much. Now he looked back on the past few years and wondered: How had they lost sight of where they came from? And that they had actually been very fortunate to have gotten as far as they had?

Tammy had to go with Dan to the lawyer for the third meeting, the one when the bankruptcy documents had to be signed. When they sat down, the first question she asked the lawyer was, *Doesn't your job depress you?*

Depress me? Glenn said. *No, I love my job! I help people. I save people's homes, I save marriages.*

Tammy didn't feel saved. The deeper they got into the bankruptcy process, the more isolated she became. She was cut off from spending money they didn't have, from shopping or going out, and she went through what Dan saw as a sort of withdrawal. She worried about their children, about their lives changing. She didn't want them to have to give up their activities. She worried that the kids would see themselves as different from their friends, as not having as much as other families had. And she had similar concerns about her own social circle, about what their own friends and neighbors would think of them if they found out. She made Dan promise not to tell a soul about their bankruptcy.

The lawyer told them that a bankruptcy filing is public record and that their names might be printed in the local newspaper. Tammy was petrified of being exposed. She was an active parent volunteer at school and on a neighborhood committee, in addition to having a social life with friends. She worried about being seen as different, a failure, and her normal life essentially ending.

Dan started scouring the *Orlando Sentinel* to see the bankruptcy filing list. He wanted to see how easy it was to spot, what was the wording and how big was the font size. When he didn't find it for a couple of weeks, he called the paper to ask about it and was told they had recently stopped printing it. He researched other ways their bankruptcy might be publicized. What about their friends who worked in banking? Were they automatically notified of everyone in bankruptcy? Was there any way people they knew would see their names on some kind of blacklist? And what about the public record? Dan went to the bankruptcy court Web site and tried to look up cases but figured out that people at least have to go to the bother of getting a paid account and logging in to search anything. And his lawyer told him there wasn't any blacklist but that any time they applied for credit, a new job, or if they had to move or rent a home during the next decade, the bankruptcy was going to show up on their credit report.

To keep their secret as safe as possible—and also because they couldn't afford to go out much anymore—they started cloistering themselves. When they were invited out, they started making excuses:

They had other plans.

He would be working late.

They couldn't find a sitter.

They must be wondering what's become of us, why we never go out anymore, Tammy thought. She hated the lies. The coverups. But she thought telling anyone the truth would be worse for sure. She didn't want to be judged or criticized, and she expected that if anyone knew they were bankrupt, she and Dan would have to endure both judgment and criticism.

A common argument explaining the swelling of bankruptcy cases in recent years is that the stigma of bankruptcy is gone. *It's not shameful the way it used to be*, critics say. These claims are rarely accompanied by any real, live bankrupt individual or family describing their bankruptcy as a routine event. Bankruptcy attorneys, including Glenn, have described some clients who do see bankruptcy as a business decision, who don't seem ashamed and who don't talk about fearing any social consequences. These types do not make up a large percentage of the people going through bankruptcy, however. And the more they are described in public accounts, the more the rest of us misunderstand and even turn against bankruptcy and those seeking its protection.

The reality, as those who meet average bankrupt families discover, is that for most bankrupt people, the stigma, the shame, and the extreme anxiety of being found out are very much alive. In the bathroom outside of the bankruptcy courtrooms in Orlando, a box of tissues is permanently bolted to the counter. Not many people say they feel good about bankruptcy (although a feeling of relief is common), and few willingly disclose their experiences with it. This is especially true of people in Dan and Tammy's category, the overspenders. One reason is that they probably feel more culpable (*We did it to ourselves! We are failures!*) and another is that after going to extremes to keep up and fit in with a certain crowd, they don't want to be branded as different (*You don't belong here! You're not one of us!*).

That's why most of us don't think we know very many people who have been through bankruptcy. The reality is that most of us probably do know somebody in that situation, if not a friend or family member, then a neighbor, an acquaintance, or someone at work. But most of them are effectively in hiding. They are showing us one side of their lives while going through personal trauma behind closed doors.

Dan and Tammy learned that 1.6 million families per year are going bankrupt. That makes 45 percent more bankruptcies these days than there are divorces. So statistically, if you know two couples who've gotten divorced in the past year, you also know three families that have recently declared bankruptcy. Also, more people are going bankrupt now than are graduating from four-year colleges. Dan and Tammy's lawyer assured them that there are others like them. But they are invisible to Dan and Tammy, just as Dan and Tammy are invisible to them.

One researcher who studied bankrupt families reported that 61 percent of those she surveyed said they didn't want their closest friend to know about their bankruptcy. The most recent book based on the findings of the Consumer Bankruptcy Project reports that 84 percent of the bankrupt people surveyed said they would be "embarrassed" or "very embarrassed" if their families, friends, or neighbors learned of their bankruptcy. Many families contacted on behalf of my research didn't want to talk about what they have gone through, even anonymously. Other researchers have had the same difficulty. As explained in the book *The Two-Income Trap*, in a large anonymous survey conducted by the University of Michigan, "The families in the survey willingly share data about their incomes, their purchases, their debts, their investments, and scores of other financial data with the researchers. And yet, when asked about whether they had filed for bankruptcy, only about half of the predicted number confessed to a bankruptcy filing. Either the sample is badly skewed, which no researcher has claimed, or the families concealed their bankruptcy filings."

Unlike in cases of divorce, there is no support system people going bankrupt can turn to. The personal side of the event is not addressed. The common response to going bankrupt is to isolate oneself. Parents inadvertently extend the stress to their children by cutting them off from the usual support network too. As the authors explain in *The Two-Income Trap*:

> When a radical change occurs in a child's life—divorce, a move to a new city, or even the birth of a new sibling—parents typically alert other adults in the child's life, asking them to give additional support and to watch for signs of trouble. But middle-class parents don't tell the teachers, the pediatrician, the school counselor, or the babysitter that their youngster may be experiencing distress because mom and dad are on the brink of bankruptcy. This leaves children isolated, confused, and conscious that something shameful is going on. The code of silence makes it difficult for these chil-

dren to seek out friends who have lived through the same experience. Children become more isolated, cut off from their peers.
Over time, this can evolve into keeping secrets and telling lies.

Deborah Thorne, in her dissertation on the stigma of bankruptcy, writes, "I would argue that the insolvent individual has long
been a venerable lightning rod of contempt. The Old Testament
taught us this lesson: 'Evil men borrow and cannot pay it back'
(Psalms 37:21)." According to Thorne's research, bankrupt people
specifically want to keep their secret from three groups: their
friends, their employers or co-workers, and most of all their parents.
They feel ashamed and do not want to be diminished in their parents' eyes. And the secrecy slices both ways. One mother described
admonishing her son for filing bankruptcy, telling him that his
grandmothers would "roll over in their graves." Then she said to the
interviewer, "And of course I don't know if they know we did [file
too] or not. But we never said anything."

The usual network we rely on to get us through personal crises
is dismantled in the case of financial failure. Just when we need to
turn to friends and family, when we need to make honest disclosures
and hear reassurances, instead we draw up inside our shells. "When
stress is encountered, other people serve as 'buffers,'" explains a
social psychology textbook. "For example, if someone has lost a job,
friends or relatives can provide a place to stay or food to eat, along
with affection and encouragement. Support helps the person get
through a bad experience." The social psychologists cite experi-
ments showing that the relief provided by tapping into a network
and having someone listen sympathetically extends to a positive
physical effect, reducing physiological stress. The text concludes, "It
seems that confession is good not only for the soul but for the body
as well."

They also have a name for what happens when we take the oppo-
site path, when we think one thing but say or act like something else

77

is the case. Cognitive dissonance, they call it, when our private reality and public presentation don't match up. That makes most of us nervous, uncomfortable. In other words, it's stressful to live a lie.

Dan worried about Tammy's depression. He wanted to convince her that they were not horrible people. He thought that if she could just see that they weren't the only ones, that there were other people who were family-oriented and even made good money who were in the same position, she would feel better. He searched online for any kind of support group for people going through bankruptcy. To his shock, he couldn't find a single connection, anywhere to turn to for help. He asked his lawyer if he knew of anything, but he didn't. They were on their own.

Even more so, Dan was on his own. Tammy didn't want anything more to do with the bankruptcy than she absolutely had to.

Dan went to bankruptcy court alone. The thought of going through with it, and in a public forum no less, caused an anxiety attack. He thought about what it would be like to run into somebody they knew, even though anybody else would be there for the same reason and be just as surprised to be seen. He expected courtroom drama, to be personally on trial and to be questioned in an antagonistic way on every expense, every financial move he had made. He figured a judge earned about the same income he did, and he imagined the judge saying, *I make what you make, and I pay my bills. Why can't you pay yours?!* He expected to have to explain why they had been taking vacations, why they had made home improvements, how they could justify spending so much on credit. What made him most nervous was that he knew he didn't have good answers to those questions. The only thing he could say, and what he believed, was that he had honestly thought they could keep up. That the next big bonus would take care of the debts. That somehow he could handle it.

Court was nothing like he had feared. No creditors came to the meeting, the trustee was friendly, and the process all business. He responded to minimal questions, and his whole appointment was over in about one minute.

It still didn't make going bankrupt painless. As Dan got further along, he fretted more about the fallout from it. When he had checked his credit report the first night he tallied up their card debts, he had seen that his employer had run credit checks periodically. What would they think of him when the next time they looked, they found out he had declared bankruptcy? The lawyer had informed him that it is illegal for employers to discriminate against people for being bankrupt. But as a practical matter, Florida is an "at will" employment state, which means workers can be fired for any reason not expressly prohibited, so it can be difficult to argue a discrimination case. The legal protection also doesn't extend to being hired by a new employer, and employers usually do run credit checks on prospective hires.

Dan had a concrete reason to believe that he wouldn't be trusted anymore to manage a business. He had been given a preview of how his company might respond. A week before he had to be in court himself, he was sitting with his boss when they reviewed a confidential employee request for time off to attend court for a bankruptcy hearing. The boss had turned to Dan and warned him, *Keep a close eye on that one.*

Dan himself does look at people differently now. He wonders about some of their friends and the people they see: Can they afford their lifestyle, or are they too falling behind? Who else is in trouble? He thinks he recognizes the signs sometimes. He wants to say something, he wants to tell them what his family has been through, what a mistake the overspending was and how he wishes he could roll back five years of his life and do it over. He wants to grab them and look them straight in the eye and say, *You've got to stop! If from one year to the next your credit card debt has gone up, you're headed for disaster.*

Bankruptcy forced Dan and Tammy to break their cycle of overspending. According to the terms of their case, every month for five years they must pay a significant portion of their income to the court. They also must surrender any bonuses or extra payments they receive. They are living on a budget designed to cover necessities only. Dan says, "It makes you question putting money in a vending machine to buy a soda." But they are still living in the same gated community, are still mingling with the better-off Joneses, and their kids still want to go to the same summer camps as their friends.

Through church, Dan and Tammy joined a couples Bible study group. They meet once a week in their homes, rotating each week. The group's members profess support for one another, often saying how they know that if any of them needed anything at all, even in the middle of the night, they could call on anyone in the group and they would be there for one another. But Dan and Tammy won't reveal to the other couples what they are going through. "These are people we know," Tammy said. "We don't want to be viewed differently."

But they are different, and Tammy can't help but notice that. The other couples do live in much bigger houses. They drive better cars. When it's Dan and Tammy's turn to have the Bible study meeting at their home, she complains that they don't have enough space. Dan tells her to be proud of what they have, but she's embarrassed. She dreads hosting.

If only she understood how common their predicament is, how many of us are burdened by keeping up appearances when things are not as they seem.

CHAPTER FOUR

༲

Capitol Secrets

Everyone thinks you're rich!

It's a definite problem, especially when thousands of people think they know you personally. That's the position national politicians are in. Capitol Hill, when you dig down to the level of the politicians' personal lives, is in some ways a Potemkin Village: What we think we see going on is much rosier than what is actually happening.

As Jack Buechner, a former member of the House of Representatives from Missouri, put it: "The minute you're elected, you immediately become a Prince or a Princess." Everyone knows that those kinds of characters lead fairy-tale lives, that they don't have to contend with the financial problems of ordinary folk.

Jack Quinn thought his family life in western New York state was nothing extraordinary. His son came home from high school with news to the contrary.

Dad, he said, *the kids at school are saying, "Your dad's a congressman, your family must be rich!"*

Then the boy had to ask: *Are we?*

The congressman's reaction fell somewhere between amusement and frustration: *No. We're not rich. But . . . we're comfortable.*

The family was comfortable, yes, living in a four-bedroom colonial in a suburb of Buffalo. However, they were not as comfortable as some other politicians, the ones who get a lot of press for being independently wealthy. At the same time, the family was nowhere near as comfortable as people assumed they were because of Quinn's high-profile job. In that context, the family wasn't doing nearly as well as people expected.

Quinn's salary of over $130,000 per year would be considered a lot of money to most constituents in the district he represented in Congress until 2004. At first it seemed like a lot of money to Quinn too. When he was elected to the House of Representatives he was working as a town supervisor making half as much money. Not that he got into politics to make money, but he and his wife, a nurse who worked part-time, naturally thought that doubling his income would mean a respite from squeezing the budget so hard for their household of four.

That didn't quite turn out to be true. This is the inside story that even the insiders don't talk about.

It's easy to confuse fame with fortune. To their constituents, national politicians can look like they're living a fast-track life of paid-for travel, cushy benefits, elaborate dinners with other high-powered people, a stream of luxurious gifts and lucrative gigs on the side.

The media encourage this image, with headlines like "Congress's Millionaires—A Thriving Breed" (*U.S. News and World Report*) and "Lawmakers Don't Feel Your Pain" (*Houston Chronicle*). Al Gore's campaign consultant said average people view Capitol Hill as "the Gucci scene." Former Nebraska senator Bob Kerrey used to bristle when constituents would tell him "You don't live in the real world

like I do." When Sam Gejdenson, a former representativ
Connecticut, was in office and locals saw him pushing his shopping
cart while buying groceries at the discount warehouse, he would be
asked, *You do your own shopping?!*

As with many misperceptions, it starts with a kernel of truth.
Some members of Congress *are* independently wealthy and, before
a recent rule change, lobbyists really did treat lawmakers to lavish
dinners on a regular basis. But for the most part, the public concep-
tion of what life is like for the legislators is off. Distressingly off.
Not many members talk about the reality of their personal lives as it
relates to money. The culture of Capitol Hill is so rife with gossip,
paranoia, spin, and back-watching that even those on the inside
sometimes don't get what it's really like on the inside.

A former five-term representative, finally away from public
scrutiny, confessed, "I have *never* been so stressed about money as
when I was serving in the U.S. Congress." He wasn't talking about
managing his office budget or fundraising for campaigns. He was
talking about the same red and black juggling act that plagues most
households, with additional expenses piled on as part of the lifestyle
and obligations of being a politician.

Former Speaker of the House Tom Foley held a focus group
among constituents in Washington state and the group was asked
what they thought dinner would be like at the home of a congressman. An ironworker "responded that he would be picked up by an
enormous limousine, taken to a huge mansion in Georgetown,
seated at a fancy table laid with silverware he didn't know how to
use and served food he didn't know how to eat," Foley recounted in
an interview later. "All I could think of," Foley said, "was the
humble basement apartment I lived in while I was flying back and
forth to my district every weekend."

The benefits that legislators receive are a common source of confusion. Retirement benefits have even been the subject of mass letters being forwarded on the Internet. These claim that members of

Congress don't pay anything into Social Security or any other retirement plan, but then even after they retire they make the same salary until death. These reports are totally untrue.

It's not just amateur e-mail reports that contribute to the myths. An article in the *Tampa Tribune* talked about "platinum parachutes" for politicians. "Unlike many Americans, public servants face few financial anxieties over retirement," the article states. "From President Bush to members of Congress, political retirees' financial security is guaranteed, courtesy of the taxpayer." Legislators do have the rare benefit of both a pension and a retirement savings plan like a 401(k) that they contribute to out of their income, but that doesn't mean the money spigots are opened full force for anyone who has served in the House or the Senate. The pension benefits build up slowly over many years of service, assuming the member keeps being reelected. Like anyone, the politicians still have to set aside precious nuggets from their paychecks to fund their retirement—and many of them, like many of us, don't quite get around to making the sacrifice. "Whenever we do radio shows, people always ask questions on retirement and healthcare benefits," says Steve Tomaszewski, the press secretary for Rep. John Shimkus of Illinois. "They think congressmen are in some sort of super-special program." Which, he points out, they're not. Jack Quinn turned down his federal healthcare benefits because his wife's employer offered a more generous plan, with vision and dental and longer coverage for their children, and he heard of colleagues doing the same.

Shimkus's office was thrown by his being portrayed as one of the wealthy members of Congress after he bought a half-million-dollar townhouse in the capital. The complete picture is that he also owes a hefty mortgage on it, and he affords the payments by sharing the space with three other lawmaker tenants. Shimkus has scrimped to support his wife, a part-time schoolteacher, and three children while commuting to work in Washington. While saving up the down payment for the property, Shimkus spent two years sleeping on an air mattress in his Capitol Hill office. He wasn't the first to come up with the arrangement. The halls of Congress might get quiet in the middle of the night, but they're not empty.

Members of Congress currently make $162,100 per year (which is taxed, yes). That's a lot of money to most people, and politicians must be careful not to complain about it. That only adds to the tension. But it's not even the relatively high salary that gives the public the misimpression of an elaborate lifestyle. It's their stockpiled wealth, whether it is real or imagined. When it's real, as with senators Edward Kennedy from Massachusetts ($10 million, family trusts), Jay Rockefeller from West Virginia (at least $200 million, Standard Oil fortune heir) or Jon Corzine from New Jersey ($262 million, former CEO of Goldman Sachs), those are the exceptions. The majority of members are not independently wealthy. People in Jack Quinn's home district would spot his picture in the newspaper with Jim Kelly, quarterback of the Buffalo Bills, or the president or other luminaries. "Because of some of the company you keep," Quinn said, "by association they think you're wealthy too."

An article in the *Houston Chronicle* describing how much better off financially members of Congress are than the average American states, "For the majority of the Senate and a growing percentage of the House, that base pay is just a drop in the buckets of assets they have that make them millionaires."

Another myth is how much these politicians rake in on the side, from giving speeches, writing books, accepting free vacations, and getting other gifts and perks. How much money legislators make and the gifts they can receive are prime subjects in the "Myth Buster" section of the Congressional Institute's Web site. It explains that members of Congress are allowed to earn from outside income only up to 15 percent of their regular salary, which means they can't sign million-dollar book deals while in office or profit in other ways. They cannot accept payments for making speeches at events (they can have up to $2,000 donated to a charity instead).

Since a rule change in the mid-'90s, they cannot accept gifts over $50—that means no free meals, either—or more than $100 total worth of gifts from any one individual or organization during a year. They can, granted, make money from investments like stocks and real estate, since those are not seen as potentially causing conflicts of interest.

However, not everyone elected to be a senator or representative has an investment portfolio working for them. Some have as few assets (sometimes none) and are just as deep (or deeper) in debt as many other Americans. Even for that, though, they find themselves criticized. Check out this account in a New York newspaper: "Imagine the kind of person who might accumulate $50,000 to $100,000 in credit card debt. That person might be out of work for a year or more. He might be sick and in the hospital. She might have a gambling problem. Or the person might be a member of the House of Representatives, earning about $158,000 a year plus full health benefits, plus travel expenses and a small stipend for housing." *For shame!* we readers are meant to hiss. *There's certainly no excuse for that!* So the politicians are portrayed as being sequestered from us, the Real People, whether they have a lot of money or are in a lot of debt.

And the article above, by the way, is wrong about the housing stipend: There isn't one. It's almost excusable that the journalist didn't know that—even some of the lawmakers themselves don't realize it at first.

When Quinn asked his wife if he could run for Congress, she said yes on two conditions: They weren't going to remortgage the house to help pay for the campaign, and they weren't going to move the family from Buffalo to Washington, D.C. That was their agreement. So he got through the campaign without tapping home equity, and when he won the election they knew he would be living in Washington alone during the weeks Congress was in session. Beyond that, they didn't talk much about how it would all work out financially. He would be making a lot more money than he had been, that much they knew, so they didn't worry. Nobody had told him about the extra expenses that would eat away at his government salary.

Quinn showed up on Capitol Hill at the orientation for new members, waiting to hear how much of their living expenses in Washington would be covered. He figured they would be getting a per diem allowance, just like a businessperson gets when traveling for a company, and like many states pay their legislators when they're working in the state capital. He was shocked to find out there was no such living allowance. Members must support their home-away-from-home completely out of their personal paychecks. And unlike other taxpayers, they cannot fully deduct the cost as a business expense. Their travel back and forth to their districts is covered by an office budget, but it never covers one's spouse or children. Quinn summed up the help he'd be getting settling into the new double life this way: *"You're here! Good luck!"*

Another representative from his state advised Quinn to call the landlord of Hill House, a boxy brick apartment building close to the Capitol building where a lot of politicians live, almost as if it's a dormitory. He was lucky to get a lease on a small, rectangular studio apartment there, but he had to pay more than $700 a month for it. The monthly rent was more than the family was paying for the mortgage and taxes on their four-bedroom house back home. The attraction was that he wouldn't have to keep a car in D.C. He borrowed furniture from everyone in the family—no allowance for that, either—and his dad helped him drive the mismatched pieces to Washington in a U-Haul.

Maintaining a double residence is the biggest challenge in the personal lives of most members of Congress. They live in one city and work in Washington, D.C., midweek, or else they move their family to Washington and commute back home to work part of the time in their districts. Either way, they have one foot each in two different places, which often strains their marriages, their families, and definitely their finances. "If most people have one mortgage and boiler to work with, you have two," says former representative Sam Gejdenson. While he was in office, he lived in a borrowed fourteen-foot trailer on his parents' dairy farm in Connecticut while building a house himself bit by bit as he put together the money. Some single politicians or couples move in with their parents or a sibling in their home district as a way to free up funds to support a primary household close to the capital.

Buying or renting real estate in or near Washington, D.C., is expensive and getting more so all the time. One-bedroom apartments currently rent for $900 to $1,600 per month. That can easily amount to more than legislators are paying for their housing back home. Rent in the suburbs is less, but living there requires having a car, so it's a tradeoff.

Those whose homes are conceivably close enough to the capital, even if beyond usual commuting distance, sometimes attempt a daily commute, via train or car, while Congress is in session. Others share apartments or rent rooms in boardinghouse-type arrangements. For his Washington residence, Speaker of the House Dennis Hastert from Illinois shares a townhouse with two aides. Many other members also share local apartments or townhouses, sometimes with several of them under one roof. That can bring one's share of the monthly rent, on the low end, down to the $500 range.

One of the longest-term communal living arrangements has gained a reputation among Washington insiders. The two-bedroom townhouse even has a nickname: Animal House. It's owned by Rep. George Miller of California. He and his wife bought it for their family nearly thirty years ago, but when they decided the children would go to school back home, Miller took in roommates to help cover the cost of the second home in Washington. Since the early 1980s, long-term roomies have come and gone as they are in and out of office. One thing they have all had in common is an unwillingness or inability to disgorge large sums of money on their local residences. The three roommates each pay Miller $550 per month. If he hadn't refinanced the house, he would nearly own it outright by now, but like many Americans he has borrowed against it to raise money. The property, according to his financial disclosure statement, is worth between $250,000 and $500,000. The refinanced mortgage stands between $100,000 and $250,000, and he has a home equity loan of between $15,000 and $50,000.

It isn't luxury, oh no. The house is known for its disarray. "Friends would come by the house and they were stunned," says Gejdenson, who lived in the house for eight years. "They had these visions of a brick mansion in colonial Williamsburg."

The furniture of Animal House comprises various secondhand pieces cobbled together over the years, the window air-conditioning unit is propped up by a hunk of construction wood, and the ceiling has had leaks, even holes. Miller and Sen. Dick Durbin of Illinois each have their own bedroom, while Sen. Chuck Schumer of New York and Rep. Bill Delahunt of Massachusetts crash in the living room. Schumer used to sleep on one battered couch and then another but eventually graduated to a twin bed. There's hardly ever any food in the refrigerator besides condiments, drinks, and the occasional leftover pizza. Over the years, various infestations have been an issue: ants, flies, crickets, mice, and worse. "The rats were enormous," Durbin described, "like little cocker spaniels."

The apartment chock full of politicians was the inspiration for a sitcom proposed to CBS by humorist Al Franken, who knew that most Americans have the wrong impression of how legislators live. "Four guys sitting around in their boxers watching TV and eating fast food," he said. "The wild lifestyle of the rich and famous." Marty Russo, who when he lived in Miller's house was a representative from Illinois, was the only tenant who kept a car in town. He used to drive the others around, and when he had his tires replaced for $200 he billed $50 to each of the roomies.

It gets worse. Some members don't have any residence in the capital to call home. Instead, they sleep rent-free in their offices. This has been going on at least since Rep. Dick Armey of Texas, who eventually became House Majority Leader, started camping on a cot in the modest House gym after he was elected in 1984. The Speaker, Tip O'Neill, kicked him out, saying it was against the rules. Armey only moved as far as his own office, where he slept for the next several years.

Many others have since followed. After working late, they creep on to couches, pump up inflatable mattresses, fold out futons, and cozy up in sleeping bags. Before their staffs arrive in the morning, they restore the office spaces to working conditions and shower and shave in the House gym, or nowadays at the Gold's gym down the street.

When stories surface about the dozens of members who have set up residence in their offices, they almost always explain how the member needed a place temporarily, spent a few nights in the office out of necessity, and ended up not leaving for some time. That's how it happened for Sam Gejdenson from Connecticut (three months on a couch), John Shimkus from Illinois (two years on an air mattress), Scott McInnis from Colorado (twelve years on a couch or in his desk chair), J.D. Hayworth from Arizona (on a couch with an air mattress since 1995), and Pete Hoekstra from Michigan (on a couch since 1993). One former member who spent some nights on his office couch pointed out that the furniture in most of the offices on Capitol Hill is well worn. (Members are not allowed to upgrade furniture out of their personal funds, only out of their office budgets.) He says of his own accommodations, "I could identify every spring in that sofa." Gejdenson says the discomfort went beyond the furniture. "It was very spooky," he says. "But it's one way to save dough."

Some articles featuring the surprising arrangements note that real estate in Washington is expensive and give a single mention of the practice as "saving money," but the financial mechanics of the job are never discussed in any detail. The members themselves, when they do grant interviews on the subject, don't speak frankly about the economics. They talk about the convenience of it, saving the time of a commute, about how they work so late and are up so early: *Why leave the office at all?* Another take on it is to claim that crashing on a couch saves the politicians from getting too enmeshed in Washington and the moral grime that some constituents associate with it. That could explain why some who do own heaps of assets, like Jack Kingston of Georgia, have also taken up residence in their offices.

For Christmas, Quinn's kids bought him a television for his apartment in Washington. He put it on top of a used dresser he had painted white, and he pivoted it to face wherever he was in the apartment: the kitchen, the couch, or the bed. When his brother-in-law came to visit he announced, *I'm going to tell everyone back home how Quinn has it made! He's got a TV in every room!* Joking aside, Quinn said, that's how the stories get started. The stories of the luxurious lives that national politicians lead.

After a couple of reelections, Quinn's son, also named Jack, was in college. Jack continued to hear from his friends about the lavish lifestyle his family must be leading. *Your dad gets a ton of money for living in D.C.,* they would comment to him. "Good friends of yours, without your even knowing it, think you're wealthy," Jack says. One of his friends saw the real deal. During two summers, Jack and his friend got summer internships in D.C. Rather than rent a place of their own, the two squeezed into the studio with Quinn. The congressman got the bed, one young man took the couch, and the other set up an air mattress on the floor. "It was surreal," Jack says.

Quinn stayed in the apartment for several years, until the rent ratcheted up past $1,000 per month. Then he relocated to an apartment in the suburbs, which meant he needed to get a car. He bought a used Ford Contour, which, since he is 6'5", he had to fold himself into.

The used compact car wasn't what people expected a congressman to be driving around the capital. Buffalo Night is a big celebration on Capitol Hill every year hosted by western New Yorkers. The guest of honor one year was Marv Levy, the former coach of the Buffalo Bills. At the reception, Quinn asked Levy where he was staying and how he was getting back there. Levy planned to take a taxi to his hotel.

Nonsense, Quinn said, *I'll drive you!*

Levy accepted and asked, *Who's your driver?*

My driver?! Quinn repeated with a belly laugh. *Me! I'm my driver!*

With the congressman and the football coach stuffed into the Contour, there wouldn't have been room for a chauffeur anyway.

There's more to the financial stress of serving as a politician in Washington than supporting a second residence.

Before they have even won an election, there is the voracious appetite of the campaign trail. For members of the House, who are elected for two-year terms, the campaigning is constant. And it costs — a lot. The average contested House campaign now costs $1 million, and vying for a Senate seat can cost more than $10 million. Headlines about these expenditures contribute to the stereotype that politicians are high rollers. "The whole thing seems suspect," Gejdenson says of the public's point of view. "You're paying $1 million for a job that pays $160,000 a year."

Fundraising is a must for those who are not independently wealthy. That means spending time with the people with the money. For politicians who come from working-class backgrounds, the fundraising aspect of campaigning can expose them to a new social scene, which revolves around having money—any kind of money. ("The nouveau riche are the *worst*," one former congressman said.) It might seem glamorous to attend parties in your honor, but it's actually stressful, even humiliating. The constant, uncloaked begging for others to help pay for your expenses is so distasteful to some politicians that they drop out of the field altogether.

A new candidate can't seriously campaign while working full time, so most of them quit their jobs. The families must get by without that paycheck for a year or more before they even know if they'll have a new job in Congress. The family budget often has to be supplemented by digging into personal savings. That is, if there are any savings. Otherwise it falls entirely on the spouse to keep supporting the family, and most also have to take on debt. Whether borrowed money is used to cover living expenses or campaign expenditures, debt is practically a necessity for middle-class politicians. It is typical for them to take second mortgages on the family home, get personal bank loans, and use credit cards.

Even in office, politicians, too, build up credit card balances. The most recent financial disclosures showed forty-three members of the House carrying credit card balances over $10,000. Rep. Tim Bishop from New York attributed his $25,000 to $60,000 credit card debt to the cost of campaigning after leaving his job in academia. "The story is that unless you are a millionaire it is awfully tough to run for Congress and be successful at it," he said. When representatives Jan Schakowsky and Melissa Bean from Illinois each revealed credit card balances of over $20,000, the Illinois Republican party issued a press release asking, "How can we trust Bean and Schakowsky to spend the taxpayer's money responsibly when their own fiscal house is in disarray?" Even if we don't think like that directly, most of the public as well as the media are completely ignorant about the reality of the personal finances of politicians.

If they do win their elections, and the whole family moves, that usually means the trailing spouse must give up his or her job back home. Employers in D.C. are often reluctant to hire politicians' spouses because they might be there for only two years, pending reelection, if the member serves in the House, or because of real or perceived conflicts of interest. That further contributes to loss of income.

Income that is earned is nipped at by myriad expenses that come with serving in Congress. It starts with getting to Washington, D.C., to start the job. Many new legislators are shocked to learn that not only is there no housing allowance for working in Washington, there's no allowance for moving expenses either. That's all paid for out of pocket. Some families drive their belongings themselves to minimize costs. Others relocate just as a squirrel stashes acorns, bit by bit with a lot of back and forth. On each trip from the home district, another suitcase of belongings is carried to D.C. One member was embarrassed at the D.C. airport's baggage claim when his suitcase popped open and pots and pans came tumbling out.

When senators and representatives are going back and forth between Washington and their home districts on business, the expenses are covered by their official office allowance. Everything else is out of pocket, including tickets for family members and any travel that is not strictly business, which includes trips for fundraising. Those add up quickly.

When you're a politician representing the people, the people need to be impressed, constantly. Appearances need to be kept up, which means wearing decent clothing and—no matter what's really going on with your finances—looking and acting like you're in complete control. There's not much fashion competition among the members themselves, but female spouses feel pressure to live up to an image. They're not so much keeping up with each other, although there is certainly some of that, as much as keeping up with expectations that they look and act the part of a celebrity. Going to receptions at embassies and being photographed at formal fundraising events, they often feel, requires a nice new outfit. Some wives cobble together their wardrobes by getting together for shopping excursions at outlets or going to consignment shops. Others are not as thrifty, even though they need to be. In either case, for those who are stretched to begin with, debt levels are quite likely to rise.

Although the perception is that politicians are constantly wined and dined, the reality is that although they can go to receptions and snack on hors d'oeuvres for as many hours and evenings as they want, sit-down meals are strictly limited by ethics rules. The $50 gift limit applies to dining too, and that is quickly exhausted at a nice restaurant. Yet lunch and dinner meetings are still part of the job—it's just that the member is often obligated to pick up the check, and sometimes not just for himself or herself. Thinking the legislators are on an expense account, dining companions frequently assume the member will take them out. When constituents visit Washington, D.C., sometimes their representative takes them to breakfast or lunch in the members' dining room and pays for it out of pocket. The rules limit what the congressional office budget can cover, and food or entertainment is never on the list. That also means that when staffs are working late or their boss wants to reward them with a pizza or sandwiches, that has to be paid for out of the lawmaker's personal money.

Contributions to charity become a big issue. Those come out of the family budget too, even though they become a professional as well as personal obligation. Seemingly every institution, club, and group in one's home district expects their elected official to support their cause. Adults think there is an expense account for it, one former representative pointed out, and kids think they're writing directly to the government for money. The requests roll in, hundreds of them every year, for donations of cash or something to be auctioned, to purchase raffle tickets or attend a fundraising event. Jack Buechner of Missouri says a standard giveaway of his was a personal tour of the Capitol building, which was economical except for the time involved, and a meal hosted by him in the members' dining room, which he tried to hold to under $50. Sometimes he gave American flags that have flown over the Capitol building—those are popular and cost a member only around $20.

Charities don't seem to fathom that a member of Congress could be battling personal budget problems. When they are turned down, which becomes an absolute necessity in many cases, "No matter what you say, people will be ticked off at you," Buechner says. "Either you feel blackmailed to give money you don't want to give, or you're viewed as a cheapskate and an ingrate. It has the potential to become a major expense, or a major public relations expense. Either way, you pay."

Even though everyone has an equal vote, Congress is in one way rather divided: those who are independently wealthy and those who are not. Among those living on their salaries alone, there are hints of envy of their peers who self-financed their campaigns and are able to live a higher lifestyle from investment income.

Besides the financial disclosures, the public documents detailing their assets, liabilities, and gifts that members have to file each year, they can tell (or they think they can tell) who's who by how everyone talks when they're hanging around the floor of the Senate or House. Quinn, for instance, often talked about his kids back home in Buffalo, about their group camping trips with other families. Others chatted in their circles about jetting off to ski weekends or to vacations in Paris.

While some of the members are sharing grungy apartments or bunking in their offices, others are living on virtual estates in Virginia and Maryland. The better-off members whose families are living back home can afford to fly them in for visits whenever they want to. Quinn and his wife, on the other hand, had to limit their time on the phone each night so they didn't run up their long-distance bill. When there was an argument or plenty to talk about and Quinn called back once or twice, his wife, whom he calls "the finance minister," had to cut him off: *Get off the phone! Save it for tomorrow!*

On the rare occasion Quinn's family came to visit in Washington, they went out for pizza or sometimes to an Irish pub. They couldn't afford to eat at the well-known Palm restaurant or Morton's of Chicago steak house where the wealthier politicians were known to dine.

A representative who had lost a previous bid for Congress was ecstatic to arrive with his wife in Washington. They felt totally ready for the go-go lifestyle: meeting people, attending events, entertaining. They rented half of a townhouse, two bedrooms and two baths, in a nice neighborhood, and stocked it with their special china and stemware from home. They brought their leased German luxury car to town. They bought some clothes that were finer than what they were used to wearing in their home state. The last thing on their minds was a budget. "We just sort of jumped in and were pretty optimistic," he says.

In a matter of weeks, they realized they were in too deep financially. Their cash flow was negative. After having spent their savings on the campaign, they didn't have reserves to support them. They could no longer afford to pay school tuition out of income and had to borrow for it. When a tax bill came due, the couple took a loan from Dad. They sold their three-bedroom house back home to get equity out of it and pay down debt. Within months they found someone else to take over the lease on the D.C. townhouse, while they downsized to the most spartan one-bedroom apartment they could find. The dishes for guests who weren't going to come—there turned out to be no time for dinner parties anyway—had to be shipped back. They felt as if they were living in student housing and jostled for time in the small bathroom. "It had a pedestal sink," the politician recalled glumly after reminiscing about the master bath in the house they had to sell back home. "There was no place to put anything."

They essentially went undercover with their new frugal lifestyle. When they had arrived in Washington, what the representative's new colleagues and staff saw were the townhouse and the luxury car. They must have figured he was one of the members who had plenty of money. "There was some bullshit that went on," the former representative admits. "People assumed I had money, and I didn't want to let them know I was struggling." He became friends with another representative who was apparently well off. "Maybe he didn't have money either," he says. "But we both talked to each other like we did."

Behind the scenes, the family's financial situation was adding significant pressure to an already high-tension way of life. He stressed over making the monthly $600 car payment. "We couldn't get out of it," he says of the multiyear lease. "It really saddled us. I wanted to get rid of that thing in the worst way." Be careful what you wish for: After they moved to the small apartment and had to jockey for parking on the street, the car was stolen.

"Nobody teaches you to be a member of Congress," the former representative says. "They don't talk about these issues. I guess because if you have enough moxie and talent to get elected to Congress, you should be able to work this out. If somebody had just said 'Take a deep breath. Talk to somebody about rentals and costs, and think it through.'"

Nobody in the know gives that advice, though. Everyone keeps the secret to themselves. It is of utmost importance to politicians that they present the right image to the outside world. "In Washington, appearances are four-fifths of the game," says Rep. Bill Pascrell from New Jersey. That means impressing the media, the public, and occasionally even one another. They're being watched. They're being judged. The walls of Washington are built with ears. At the office you're being observed by your mostly young, admiring staff. In the home district, you're being followed by constituents. In either place, you're likely to be trailed by reporters. Your every move, at almost any moment, is possibly being monitored, recorded, talked about. Your image and your reputation—and therefore your job—are at stake. "You live in a glass bowl," Buechner says, "and the sooner you learn that, the better."

Regarding their personal finances, most politicians adopt the unofficial policy of the less said the better. If you're independently wealthy, you'll want to work at playing the average Joe, because you don't want to seem out of touch with reality. Yet if you're pinched, if you're as stretched financially as most Americans, you can't exactly admit that, either. "You can't whine about making $125,000," says one former member. "You can't talk about it publicly, and you can hardly talk about it privately." The current salary of $162,100 is nearly four times the median household income in America. If you complain about financial problems, if you try to delineate how much your life is costing and why you're not quite managing to live within your means, you'll get accused of being out of touch.

"It's the bastard child at the family reunion," Buechner says of money. "When you're in the upper 1 percent of wage earners in the United States, and asking people to give you the job, you're reluctant to talk about something like how much it costs. That's a pretty nervous vein to strike."

The press can ask about it, but they won't get answered. Politicians don't want to be on the record unspooling a tale of financial woe. Even if confidentiality is promised, it's too delicate a topic to take the risk. *What if somebody figured out who was talking? Why start the rumor mill churning?* Besides, there are the facts to contend with: Members are making huge salaries compared with the majority of Americans. "If I were to explain this situation as I am now," says the former member who had to downsize out of the townhouse, "I'd probably get criticized for not managing my affairs well." Both the press and constituents are getting by (or not) on much less. So there's no question of sympathy from them, because there won't be any.

Sam Gejdenson recalls that after he voted for a pay raise in Congress, a television reporter spit out the sarcastic question, *Come on, Congressman, you didn't need that raise to feed your children, did you?!* Gejdenson, who was always short on money, was so offended by the question that years later he's still stewing about it. But he hadn't tried to set the reporter straight. "I bit my tongue," he says.

It's an art that politicians must perfect: the polished appearance. The front. We're all doing it to a degree—sanitizing our images—but they are the professionals. Even after they're out of office, the paranoia and defense mechanisms linger. When I was talking with Jack Quinn, even though he was trying to be completely open and honest, the politician in him frequently popped up, making disclaimers for the record. The battle between presenting the truth and presenting an image played out again and again:

When describing his surprise at there not being a living allowance: "Not to complain! I knew what the job paid," Quinn said. "Being a member of Congress is the greatest job in the United States."

After describing being surrounded in Washington by people with lots of money: "Since we didn't run for Congress to make money, it worked out fine. We never wanted for anything."

Talking about how, despite people thinking they were wealthy, the family didn't have much in savings, his wife shopped at Kmart, and family vacations were spent camping in state parks: "We never talked about it, because who can complain about making over $150,000 a year? We had everything we needed."

Discussing retiring from Congress to become a lobbyist making three times as much money: "Money didn't come up a lot in the discussions [with his wife] of whether to change [jobs]." Just as I was thinking *Nonsense!*, his next statement was, "Of course, we did talk about money."

Of course the couple talked about money—quite a bit, behind closed doors. Because everyone must manage their personal finances as well as figure out how much is necessary or safe to reveal to the outside world. It's a tradeoff. The more honest you are, the more you tell the naked truth, the more opportunity you will have to commiserate with others in similar situations. However, the more you reveal, the more vulnerable you make yourself to criticism. Better to suffer alone, behind the scenes, than to open yourself up to misinterpretation and possibly being portrayed as incapable, ungrateful, or even unfit for public office.

The accepted social wisdom is to avoid any semblance of squawking. That's even true on the inside, among members themselves. The culture of Capitol Hill revolves around the pressure of performing your job and holding on to your seat. Avoiding personal money as a topic starts before the politicians even get to town. More than one former member described how the financial strains came as a complete surprise to them and their families. "As a candidate, you think what everyone else thinks: that congressmen make a lot of money and it's a great life," says the spouse of a former representative. "When you talk to members and former members, you're talking about strategy and how to get there. You're not even thinking about how it'll be when you get there. You just want to get there."

On the Hill, when personal money does comes up, it's water

cooler talk, mentioning a child going off to college and that being expensive or whatnot. It's not about mechanics, not about the personal pressure. Just as they insulate themselves from outsiders, they also insulate themselves from one another. They don't know a lot about what's going on with one another's finances, beyond realizing who has outside money and who doesn't, and when they do hear of shortages there isn't much sympathy. They're all being paid the same, they reason, and they all have to make it work. Their personal finances are almost expected to be the last thing on their minds (which is one reason that day-to-day responsibility for managing them is usually outsourced to the spouse, when there is one). "There's as much talk of that as there would be among twenty middle-aged guys sitting around talking about impotency," Buechner says. "You just don't do it."

Besides, there is the natural tendency toward avoidance. You feel financial stress but don't want to deal with it, maybe not even admit it to yourself. "You have to have an ego to run for these jobs," Buechner says. "People tell you all the time how special you are. And while they're telling you how special you are, you don't want to change the subject and talk about how ordinary you are, and that *I can't afford to have this job*."

Although nobody runs for Congress for the paycheck, some do decide to give it up because of financial pressure. "If you don't have family money and are honest, which most are," a former representative says, "you don't have the opportunity to build wealth while you're in office." Some leave Capitol Hill looking for high-paying positions in the private sector, which some can get and others can't. The stereotypical money-making route is to become a lobbyist. The field is competitive, and not as many former legislators go into lobbying as many people think. As before, it's the few super-high earners who get the headlines.

After twelve years in office, Jack Quinn had earned retirement benefits of $22,400 per year, to start at retirement age. Since his wife had been working part-time, she hadn't built up any retirement account. After his working as a politician and their raising a family and helping the kids through college, the couple, approaching their midfifties, hadn't squirreled away much savings.

He gave up his seat in the House by not running for reelection. From among several offers, he chose a job as a lobbyist for a salary of about $500,000. (That sounds high—until you find out that some of his peers who became lobbyists have cracked seven figures.) He's reluctant to say that financial considerations played much of a role in the decision, but he says his family's lifestyle still hasn't changed much. He does concede that he and his wife can go out to dinner more now ("Nothing fancy!" he insists), and that they are helping their children with student loans, paying off bills, and, for once, building up savings. "We believe we have another chapter to work. Now that I think about it," he says, "this phase of our life might be to help us prepare for retirement."

People might have assumed he was rich all along, but now, despite the high income, Quinn and his wife are in the same perilous position as so many Americans their age: piecing together their nest egg just a few years away from what would be retirement.

CHAPTER FIVE

༄

Baby Boomers Beware

There is something pretty big that they don't tell you in school. We don't talk about it among ourselves. Parents don't usually warn you about it either.

"Why would they?" Tucker asks. In his midfifties now, he has learned it on his own. "Who's going to tell you that when you're younger? If they did, you'd say 'That sounds too hard!'"

At some point it just scrapes against you. And you have to handle it, however you can. Privately. What they don't tell you is: *The money won't always be there.*

At first Tucker never really thought about money. Or what he was going to do with his life. Or how he would get by. That was the thinking as the baby boomers grew up: *There are so many opportunities. Things will just work out.* Nobody was nervous.

His parents had been nervous while Tucker was growing up. His father came back from World War II and bounced around a little, unsure of a career path. He ended up working for Tucker's grandfather, selling insurance. Tucker's mother was a columnist for the local newspaper until she couldn't afford it any longer. Raising three children in an industrial town in Michigan, the couple ended up needing two solid incomes. She stopped writing to earn her teaching certificate and got a job as a high-school teacher.

"That should have tipped me off," Tucker says. It should have tipped him off to the financial realities of life, to the tradeoffs. "It didn't."

On Tucker's block while he was growing up lived a manager at the local power company, a manufacturer of prefab houses, a writer. When his parents went to potluck dinners, the social set was higher end: a lawyer, a successful insurance salesman, the local shipbuilder. Some kids at school worked on their families' farms. They never had time for anything except their chores. When Tucker went to some of his friends' houses the woodwork was too dark, the wallpaper frayed. The houses hadn't been redone in years. Other friends of his parents took the back off of their house and converted the space to a work studio. Some sent their kids to music camp. Tucker didn't think through the differences among these groups.

His parents, who were college-educated, weren't strivers. They wanted the same things all the other families did in the boom after the war: a house, a car, a television. They saved for those things and paid mostly cash for them. The times they struggled with money, they never let the children see it. They knew all about anxiety and necessity from the war and the Depression, and they never wanted their children to feel at risk, to feel threatened the way they had. Tucker and his siblings were shielded. During their childhood in the 1950s and early 1960s, life seemed pretty comfortable, the world was stable, they were secure.

Tucker's parents told their children to go to college, to broaden their intellectual and cultural horizons. When Tucker got into an Ivy League school, his parents helped him pay some of the tuition. The rest of the bill he paid by working at factory jobs in the summers and by taking out student loans about equal to the price of a Ford

Pinto. His parents sent fifty dollars now and then, and it went far. He never worried a moment about the student loans he took out. He even thought, *Fuck it. If I default, what can they do to me?*

"I thought for about fifteen minutes about what I wanted to do with my life after graduation," Tucker says. "I just said, *That stuff will take care of itself.*"

It didn't.

Baby boomers have had high expectations from the beginning. It's not just their large numbers that make them different as a generation (about 76 million born between 1946 and 1964). Unlike their parents, who had been deprived during the Depression and war years, the boomers were born into the post–World War II euphoria. The economy roared, more women entered the workforce, and by the mid-1950s for the first time white-collar workers outnumbered blue-collar workers. The average American family prospered, many with two incomes, and embraced a new suburban, consumerist lifestyle.

Children were a focus of attention, even indulged. *Dr. Spock's Baby and Child Care* first came out in 1945 and deemphasized punishment. The architecture of houses featured more open, shared living spaces that allowed family togetherness. The boomer children were the first generation to grow up with television. As they came of age, housing became more affordable and higher education more inclusive and accessible. By the mid-1960s, nearly 40 percent of high-school graduates were going on to college, more than twice the amount that did so in their parents' generation.

"We were steeped in a mentality that you could do and be whatever the hell you wanted to be," says Scott Wetzler, a baby boomer who is now a psychologist. "We were the generation that was going to define things. The world revolved around us."

Beyond the usual adolescent pulling away from parents, the early boomers mastered rebellion. They were gregarious, competitive, and free-spirited, eager to make their own way in the world—and determined to have it their way. Known as the Now Generation and the Me Generation, they adopted in the '60s the mantra *Don't trust anyone over 30.*

When Tucker was in high school, *Time* magazine made the generation their "Man of the Year" for 1966. The cover story exalting everyone under twenty-five described them like this:

> That generation looms larger than all the exponential promises of science and technology . . . Never have the young been so assertive or so articulate, so well educated or so worldly . . . This is not just a new generation, but a new kind of generation . . . [The baby boomer] has a unique sense of control over his own destiny . . . Science and the knowledge explosion have armed him with more tools to choose his life pattern than he can always use: physical and intellectual mobility, personal and financial opportunity, a vista of change accelerating in every direction. Untold adventure awaits him. He is the man who will land on the moon, cure cancer and the common cold, lay out blight-proof, smog-free cities, enrich the underdeveloped world and, no doubt, write finis to poverty and war.

But no pressure.

Another catchphrase the boomers adopted in their youth: *Tell it like it is.*

As the boomers are today becoming the patriarchs of society, they're having more trouble than anyone with that dictum. Not every boomer, even the college-educated ones with the intellect and promise described by *Time*, has been able to live up to the expectations that both they and society had of their generation. As they turn fifty and square off to reality, especially when it comes to the shortfall in their personal finances, the letdown can be crushing. Not that many of them talk about it.

Even if Tucker didn't have high expectations of what he wanted to achieve with a career—he had vague notions of working with language in some way—others did have high hopes for him. In his senior year at college he won a Rhodes scholarship, perhaps the most prestigious award available to students in the United States. The highly competitive scholarship is awarded to a handful of students from each region of the country every year and covers all of their expenses for graduate school at Oxford in England. Rhodes scholars are expected to be the leaders of their time, in whatever their field of endeavor. Tucker studied English.

When he returned from England he got a job as an editor at a commercial publishing house. The higher ups were impressed by his background, especially that he was a Rhodes scholar, and he was told he was being groomed for great things. He liked the idea of working in publishing, and he saw the opportunities: to move up, to make much more money, and eventually to write his own books.

He was impatient, however. He had to play the game of climbing the corporate ladder, and he wasn't up for it. The Now Generation wasn't about making long-term plans and following them. Life was more about the liberty of the moment. That's what Tucker and his friends had talked about in college, and he wasn't giving up on it.

Not happy at work, and earning barely enough money on which to get by, Tucker decided to test the situation. He went in to see his boss.

I've been here for a year, he said. *Let's talk about compensation. I do a lot of things, I'm working hard, I think I deserve a raise.*

The boss saw the situation quite differently.

One, you're not happy here, he said. *And two, we publish books, and you haven't published any!*

Tucker explained why he had passed over every manuscript that had come to him: *I haven't seen anything good!*

He left the meeting without a raise, and without a job.

What he wanted to do, it was more clear than ever, was to write. Tucker went back to graduate school, in the Ivy League, with a fellowship and by taking on more student loans. Again the financial commitment didn't concern him. It would be doable. It would work out.

Grad school didn't go smoothly, though. The teachers didn't give him the kind of feedback he thought he had signed up for. His girlfriend kicked him out of their apartment. His brother was killed in an auto accident. All within a few months of being fired from the only real job he'd ever had.

It wasn't a time of mentors and encouragement. Nobody had answers for him about how to do what he wanted to do. He started to feel like an outsider. Classmates from college and Oxford seemed to be on straightforward, upward career paths. They went to graduate school and became academics, they went to law school and became lawyers, they entered the military and became officers. All around him, others his age were moving up, up, up.

It's not that everyone was really doing better than Tucker. The challenge, as usual, is the pond. Within the mass of baby boomers, as with every generation, were subgroups of lesser and greater expected potential. Those with college educations, then as now, are expected to be high achievers, the leaders, the most successful and stable in their careers and their finances.

Once you've graduated from college, your classmates make up a ready pool of comparison. Their achievements come in waves—and keep on coming and keep on coming. As a member of the Class of 1977 said of graduating from Harvard, "It's a tyranny. It hangs over you the rest of your life. Did you live up to it?"

Others in your class sure seem to be living up to it. They make sure you notice their every step up, because they are the ones who write in to the Class Notes column of the alumni magazine. If there were ever a forum predisposing us to share good news, Class Notes is it. "You hear from people who want to brag," says an Ivy League correspondent of the Class of 1978. "It's a fascinating issue: the bourgeois panic that goes on as people try to one-up." Writer Daphne Merkin, a 1975 graduate of Barnard College in New York, describes reading her class's alumni notes "with a mixture of rabid curiosity and an apprehension bordering on dread."

Tucker went to a reunion of Rhodes scholars a few years after returning from England and found it upsetting. He came dressed casually, the others wore suits. The lawyers in the group, even in their twenties, talked about cases and addressed each other as "counselor." He didn't have much to say about his own career. After that he didn't bother keeping in touch for many years. He preferred not to know.

We're supposed to get over that phase in life, the keeping track and keeping up. Graduates who have been out in the world for a couple of decades or more like to say they and their classmates have matured, that later in life it's less about accomplishment and competition and more about meaningful relationships. *Hmmm.* That sounds good, but unfortunately not everyone gets past the competition stage. Witness some evidence from these Ivy Leaguers past their twenty-fifth reunions:

Actual note: "I'm teaching Chaucer to undergraduates and Plato, Aristotle, Nietzsche, Derrida, et al. to the graduate students . . . I'm preparing to apply to graduate schools for a second PhD in computer science this fall." (Class of 1978)

Actual note: "My hobbies include culinary arts, sports and rare cars." (Class of 1979)

Actual note: "I have unfortunately not yet realized my lifelong ambition to open a water ski school, but instead I have acquired three advanced degrees and held a succession of high-powered information technology positions in government, insurance, publishing and banking." (Class of 1971)

Occasionally there's a tension-breaking reality check from inside the ranks, like this one:

Actual note: "After lo these many months of reading about classmates' successes and triumphs, I am aligning some recycled electrons to provide an update . . . Authored no books, wrote no papers, chaired no committees, received no awards. It's been a full life." (Class of 1971)

For those under the spell of a competitive spirit, nothing will stoke it like learning of the latest career milestone reached by a classmate, someone who by definition had very similar opportunities as you and the exact same amount of time to take advantage of them. College classmates, at least some of whom are going to do *very* well, can turn into a sickening comparison cohort. Merkin explains the keeping-up-with-classmates phenomenon this way: "It involves what I can only call a Machiavellian form of emotional accounting, the sort of bottom-line, three-o'clock-in-the-morning realizations that leave one inwardly gasping, *Is this my life?*"

Accomplishments of any sort can inspire envy, but our standard measure of success is still money. That is the missionary position of social comparison. At least it is for the men. "It's disproportionately weighted, regardless of the needs it's supposed to fulfill. It really is a way of keeping score," says Scott Wetzler, who in his psychology practice in New York sees male patients, even those with seven-figure incomes, wrestle with feeling financially inferior.

Since subsistence-level food, shelter, and clothing are pretty much givens for the majority in the United States, accumulating money has almost become a primal instinct. "Self-preservation anxieties from our caveman days have been transferred onto finances," Wetzler says. Fighting for our physical lives doesn't happen much anymore, but fighting for financial security does, daily. Even the baby boomers have succumbed to concern over money. "Financial security is what made the world a safe place for us," Wetzler says. "When our finances are bad, that's when we feel threatened."

But almost nobody is showing it. That has become part of the survival strategy.

Tucker dropped out of graduate school. He was sleeping on a friend's couch, with three people crowded into the apartment, dorm-style. Again he looked for a job, but this time around it was more difficult to get in the door. He had been fired from his latest job and walked out of a graduate program. Still, with an Ivy League degree and a Rhodes scholarship on his résumé, he heard the "you're overqualified" line a lot.

Months went by and he wasn't employed. His parents helped him scrape by. For the first time lack of money became a reality for him, but he still managed not to think about it. Finally he found a job in publishing. It was a major step down the totem pole from where he had been before. He worked as a copyeditor and, in his words, the job sucked.

He did, however, meet the woman whom he would marry. She was also working in publishing, and she also didn't love her job. He moved into her apartment. They commiserated about being stuck working for money. After a few months of talking about this problem, they looked at each other and said, *Fuck this! We're out of here!* They quit their jobs, and with a little money she got from her parents, they disappeared for two months to New England to write.

The time spent writing during their escape was like a honeymoon, blissful. She got a good start on a novel. He wrote drafts of various stories but didn't complete anything. They loved this writing life, except that all honeymoons eventually end. They returned to the city, and reality hit hard.

He was getting minimal help from his parents, who couldn't afford much. Her parents were well off and weren't going to let her starve, but they weren't going to support her, either. He freelanced for the publishing company he had worked for and wrote some low-paying book reviews.

It wasn't enough to pay the rent and get groceries. They counted pennies. They never ate at a restaurant. They didn't go to the movies. Tucker rode his bike everywhere to save bus or train fare. If he saw a book he wanted being sold used for less than a dollar, he still passed it up.

Their lives revolved around the issue of money, and not having it. "It became totally real," Tucker says. They needed money, and quickly. They talked about it all the time. They argued over it. Both wanted to be writers, but they had to ask each other, *How are two of us going to do this if neither is very successful at it?*

It became a Darwinian struggle, especially after they married. His wife insisted that she had a real project in gear with her novel, so he had to be the one to go out and get a steady job. He didn't exactly agree, but there was no denying that making money was an absolute necessity.

Again he was looking for work, and again his search had to slip into less and less desirable jobs. He ended up at an hourly job at a local college, as a tutor in a program for underprivileged students. He was making less than he'd been making in publishing. He worked a lot of hours, but it still wasn't enough to pay for the basics.

He kept that job and looked for a second one. He landed a year-long research fellowship at a library. The two incomes together finally brought in enough money to live on without constant worry. However, there was a tradeoff. "Now I was a working person," Tucker says. "What I wanted to do, which was to be a writer, was going to be very difficult." He and his wife diverged down two separate paths: She became the novelist, he became more of a worker bee.

He had opportunities for more stimulating jobs. Like one at a respected national institution. He got far in the interview process, the job was virtually given to him . . . but then he didn't get it. He was crestfallen, and mystified. Tucker didn't understand how the world was working, why it was so difficult for him to get what he wanted. "I had no idea things weren't always as they seemed. You don't get things you think are yours, things fall through. That's the way things go. But I was clueless. I took it personally."

The bits of writing he was squeezing in on the side weren't going well, either. Two or three longer pieces of literary criticism that he wrote, unpaid, were killed as the publications went to press. Tucker was disappointed enough to give up most of his attempts at writing anything for publication.

For their wedding, his fiancée's parents had bought them a house. So they were able to live without having to make a rent or mortgage payment. That became a permanent saving grace in their financial lives. The house was a fixer-upper, however, and the repairs were their own responsibility. It had plumbing problems. The electrical wiring was faulty. Doors didn't fit. For that matter, some of the walls didn't fit. Tucker and his wife got work done cheaply by doing it themselves and stretching it out over the years. For furniture they found usable stuff on the street. They'd pick an interesting chair frame off the curb and reupholster it themselves.

In addition to taking care of the needy property, the couple was expecting a baby. With that responsibility, Tucker needed a traditional, well-paying job. He looked in publishing again, but what he needed was an editor's job and he didn't have enough experience for that. What he found was a position working in communications for a company located in a downtown office tower. At last he was making what he considered decent money, about $24,000 in the early '80s. He was being paid a professional salary and receiving full benefits, including a retirement savings plan.

It felt good, for once, to have enough money. He had cash in his pocket, and he could spend it. One of the first things Tucker did was venture into a chichi boutique near his office. He spotted a leather Bottega Veneta purse. It was expensive, but he knew his wife would love it. She did.

For years they had been dragging around a small television passed down from his parents. It barely worked. They discussed getting a new one, nothing big, just enough to see the picture clearly. Tucker went to the electronics store and realized he could afford a full twenty-incher. He put down the money, hailed a cab, and took the big TV home.

For the first time in his life, he started shopping for clothes. After work he would wander through chic stores he never would have thought to enter before. He targeted beautiful items, waited for them to go on sale, then made the purchases.

Money made life *easier*. They had another baby and could afford to hire part-time help with childcare or support an au pair with room and board. Since Tucker had two and later three weeks of paid vacation, the family could travel. They had friends living in Europe and took them up on visiting. They even bought some new furniture.

However, the income came at a cost. Tucker had to hustle out the door for the morning commute. He worked from 9:30 in the morning until 6:30 or 7:00 at night. There was always more to do at the office than he had time to get done. It wasn't the stifling corporate environment he had always dreaded becoming a part of, but he was still too tired after work to get any writing done.

He had lawyer friends who were already making six figures. Although further behind them, Tucker was on the money-making trail. Very quickly, he was making more money than his father had ever made. After a few years he had moved up to vice president; he was making $50,000 and was poised to make much more if he stayed on as an executive. Every year he got bonuses. Earning more and more money felt great. He could see how people got hooked on it. The routine got its tentacles around him, and he worked for a salary for half a decade.

Each day he worked at the office, though, he had the same thought. It would come to him at some point during the day, often as he was packed into a train during rush hour: *What am I doing? Am I ever going to be a writer?*

Tucker had started life out with the notion that he could do what he wanted to do, and he refused to let go of that ideal because of needing money. There had to be a way to balance the two.

Years before, as an undergraduate student, he had been demonstrating and confronting the police and chanting '60s slogans about the country being corporate and corrupt and about people leading narrow, morally bankrupt lives. After a few years at an office job, he realized how true it all was. Some people were energized by their jobs, but not Tucker. The work didn't engage him, and he struggled with it. He still didn't know how to play the game. He couldn't put up a front for the sake of progressing in his career.

He felt suffocated. He realized, as he was supporting two children and a wife, how his parents' generation had fallen into the patterns he had criticized and rejected as a student: It was out of necessity. The idea of living free and things just working out? That just wasn't the reality. He felt the pressure to support a family and a lifestyle, and that pressure was never going to go away. Disappointment set in. "I had no inkling things were going to be like this," Tucker says. "It all relates to money."

He could still make a choice. He could give up the well-paying job with the benefits. He would be going back to financial insecurity, in exchange for a return to writing. That was still the tradeoff, and there wasn't any way around it. It was never going to *just work out*. He had to choose between security and freedom.

At thirty-seven years old, he chose freedom. He quit the job. His plan was to continue working on a freelance basis, and the boss went for it. The first year, his income dropped about 20 percent, and the family's expenses went up because he had to pay for things like their health insurance. When he left the job he took a check for the $4,000 that had accumulated in his retirement account. It melted into living expenses. He no longer set aside any of his income for retirement.

The money stress returned, and it would never go away again. Their account ran dry before the end of the month. They had to borrow money to pay taxes. The familiar arguments came back. His wife, who continued to write fiction and was taking care of the children, questioned whether he was making enough for his freelance work. They didn't have money for indulgences, not for clothes, sometimes not even for books. They opened a home equity line of credit to make up for frequent shortfalls. Their lifestyle consisted of robbing Peter to pay Paul.

But Tucker was writing again. In between the work he had to do to get paid, he got some things published, and it made him proud.

"All of this stuff is more complicated than I ever imagined," he says. "But you have to figure it out."

The baby boomers, generally, have not done a very good job of figuring it out. They themselves don't even know how to think about where they've ended up. We hear, from the media, about two sides of the generation: The first is that they're the most prosperous generation ever, controlling sacks of assets and about to inherit even more, and ready to spend lavishly on go-go retirement years. The second is that they're totally unprepared to support themselves in retirement and are headed for doom as Social Security buckles under their bulk and they haven't saved enough of their own to live on. Both sides are true of groups within the generation. What is interesting is that a boomer can fit into one group and still feel or act as if they fit into the other.

Tucker and his wife, as their property value appreciated and together they eventually reached a household income double the median amount for their state, entered society's upper echelon—at least statistically. They are in better shape than most others their age. However, psychologically they are almost as anxious about the future as the boomers who will likely have to rely on monthly Social Security checks.

The boomers, in their peak earning years, are making more than anyone. They also control a lot of assets. As with the country as a whole, however, the wealth is far from divvied up evenly. The boomer generation is the most bifurcate of all, with the money bunched up at the top. And the rich really do get richer: The generation is coming into at least a $1 trillion collective inheritance over the next decade, which will be staying with those at the top who have been well off all along. Despite headlines about the massive wealth transfer that make it sound as if boomers are about to win some kind of lottery, most inheritances in America are less than $25,000. And as *American Demographics* starkly announced, "The vast majority of boomers will never inherit a single dime."

The boomers are an affluent generation, but they're big spenders rather than savers. The early boomers spend more on new cars, entertainment, and household furnishings than any other group. *Time* magazine recently reported on boomers taking their families to Canyon Ranch or on extended Mexican cruises to celebrate the holidays instead of hosting at home. They are putting pools on their properties like there's no tomorrow.

Like there's no tomorrow. That's the only way the equation balances: The baby boomers can spend so much because many of them have been living at or beyond their means. Remember the environment that the first wave of boomers was born into: one of prosperity, security, plenty. As they got older, they didn't necessarily shed that Now Generation mentality. They have generally been able to indulge themselves by sacrificing savings and relying on debt. The more senior boomers have higher credit card balances than any other age group.

A report written for those who sell pools characterized boomer customers like this: *"I've got money—sort of.* Baby boomers are indeed a huge economic prospect for anyone in sales-oriented fields. Yet, many boomers really aren't in the financial position to buy pricey durable goods but will do so anyway, according to demographers." They're not overspending to keep up with each other as much as to keep up with their own expectations of what they deserve, no matter what the reality of the circumstances.

The boomers have a completely different attitude toward debt than their parents had. Tucker describes what debt meant to his parents: "It meant you had to go to the bank and say 'It's not working. Can you help me?' It meant foreclosure. It meant failure." To his generation, on the other hand, it has become a tool. "We use debt to finance our operating expenses," Tucker says.

As the boomers age they are more likely to take on additional debt than to pay it off and increase their savings. It's not all because of an overly optimistic attitude about living for the day. Some of the trouble stems from a shift in demographics. More boomers had children later in life than did previous generations, either the first time around or as second families. A think tank recently noted that the timing "pushes high-cost expenditures like higher education, family housing, and dependent health care closer to retirement age. For each of these expenditures, there is a correlating form of debt on the rise: college debt, mortgage debt, credit card debt."

In addition to having children later, boomers are holding on to them longer. "Permaparenting," supporting children financially well into adulthood, has become a trend among baby boomer parents. Boomers themselves generally couldn't wait to separate from their own parents when they came of age, but their own kids are roosting in the family nest into adulthood. The most recent census found half of all single people between 18 and 24 years old living at home with their parents. That's more than 13 million "kids," known as *boomerangers*. Their parents often let them live rent-free, and they pay the kids' health and car insurance, cell phone bill, and other expenses. They'll even help with the down payment on a house.

Even though they are being generous, the boomers again are focusing on the here and now at the expense of their own future. "Permaparents suffer potential financial and emotional repercussions," reports *Psychology Today*. "The empty-nest years are a crucial time for adults to bone up for retirement, rather than pay off their child's credit cards or feed another mouth." The president of a national credit counseling agency says more boomer-age people are asking for help in managing debt, and one reason they have overextended themselves is that they have helped their children too much.

After an adulthood of living and spending to the max, the boomers have got to keep going into what could have been retirement. Their financial obligations—helping children pay college tuition, making payments on mortgages that have been refinanced rather than paid off, taming credit card debt, shouldering healthcare expenses—make it a practical impossibility for many to stop earning. Financial planners used to estimate we would need a fraction of our current income after we retire, because some expenses, like supporting children and paying the mortgage, would have gone away by then. With the boomer generation, the ideal estimate has commonly stretched not only to matching current income but to exceeding it. Expenses are higher, lifestyles are faster, and lives are longer.

Since many boomers have managed to keep their expectations high while not preparing to support themselves in retirement, the solution, mixed with denial or panic, is to keep working and keep earning, and to hope the opportunities don't run out. Just as Tucker plans to do.

Some of the boomer rhetoric is that the generation is unstoppably energetic, that they wouldn't *want* a golden years–style retirement on the golf course. That could be partly true, but more likely we're seeing a psychological phenomenon of retrofitting: Faced with a reality, we not only adjust to it but start seeing it as what we wanted all along. It's a coping mechanism that is well suited to boomers over age fifty.

Work used to be called the pension of the poor. Now it has become a widespread strategy for even the comparatively well-off boomers, like Tucker. Even though he and his wife make a fat salary compared to others, in the context of their lifestyle it doesn't consistently cover the expenses. They haven't been setting aside income to tap later, so they don't foresee the day when they will be able to live without earning a paycheck. Multiple surveys show that the majority of baby boomers plan to keep working past traditional retirement age. In one such survey, just under half of the younger boomers and well over a third of the older boomers said they plan to do so because they need the money.

Three out of four boomers in one survey said paying for health insurance is a top financial concern. And it should be: Medical costs are rising faster than income in the United States. The country spent $250 billion on medical care in 1980 and is now spending $1.4 trillion a year. The percentage of large companies offering health insurance to retirees has dropped to a third, and considering most Americans are employed by small businesses rather than big companies, and paying for employees' health insurance is an especially onerous expense for small businesses, the vast majority of us will be paying for our insurance on our own or relying solely on Medicare.

The median net worth for families with heads of household ages 45 to 54 is $132,000. Take out the home equity portion, and the assets ring up at a median of $72,000. Among individuals in that same age range who own an individual retirement account or 401(k)–type retirement savings plan, the median balance of an IRA is $13,000 and of a 401(k) is $20,000. Half of the boomers, moreover, don't have either kind of retirement account.

A recent survey by AARP of Americans over age 45 underscores the dynamic at work. "An astounding 50 percent of all midlife and older Americans go to sleep every night concerned about having enough money to pay for basic monthly costs such as telephone, groceries and utilities," the researchers report. "We found that despite serious financial concerns among 45+ consumers, a significant number of people say they will spend money on leisure activities in the next two years." Fifty-seven percent say they'll save for retirement, while 63 percent report they'll go on vacation.

Expectations and reality just don't match up. No wonder boomers don't want to talk about this topic.

Since giving up the office job, Tucker has lived irregular paycheck to irregular paycheck. Even when the income is high, the expenses are still hard to keep up with. If he had had to make a mortgage payment all these years, he would've had to have made further sacrifices. As it is, when he has needed money for home repairs or to get by during lean periods, he has borrowed against the house, taking as much as $50,000 cumulatively from the home equity line of credit. Having to pay that back on top of covering their regular expenses puts them in a palpable pinch.

That's not what people see, though. The family looks affluent. The three children all went to private school. The neighbors must have noticed that neither Tucker nor his wife go to a regular job. Some know that she is a novelist, but few know what he does for a living, and even fewer (like none) realize how he has to scramble to make it work. Nobody has ever asked.

The biggest green flag waving is their property. To buy it today would be prohibitively expensive for anybody not making at least $500,000. Over the years, others on their block have supported the expense by renting out part of their townhouses. Many have cashed out and moved to less expensive regions. It sure must seem to observers that Tucker and his wife don't have money stress.

Tucker knows this game, the game of figuring out how other

people are getting by. He plays it himself, by sizing up situations, making assumptions, and running his own calculations. "I look at my neighbors," he says, "and ask, *How does what they say square with how they live?*" Often it doesn't. Take the family down the street. Tucker and his wife have known them for years. In that household, he is a professor, she works sporadically. They have two kids in private colleges, without scholarship funding. The house is paid off, Tucker and his wife know, but how does this couple afford the traveling that they do? They disappear to New Orleans, Paris, India—for two or three weeks at a time! And then they complain of how expensive everything is. They tell Tucker and his wife that when their son came home from college, they made him pay rent because they couldn't afford to have another person living and eating there without paying for it.

"I add all those things up and say, *Who are we kidding here?!*" Tucker says. "I don't have patience for conversations like that." There's money oozing from the family tree and Tucker knows it. That *has* to be it. They're not genuinely strapped, Tucker thinks, because he has noticed that they never say things like, *We can't afford to do that this year.* They keep traveling, they keep getting work done on the house—it's all getting paid for somehow.

Then there's a longtime artist friend. Tucker can't figure out how this guy affords his lifestyle either. He is also a world traveler, he eats out all the time, and on top of it he has purchased investment properties. A few years back, the friend talked about a gallery wanting to raise the price of his artwork, and that gave Tucker the opening to find out just how much he sells the pieces for. Tucker took the number and started calculating, backward and forward. He figured out how much art the friend has to sell to finance what Tucker guesses are his expenses. *He has to be an assembly line!* he figures. It still doesn't quite make sense to him, though, because artists don't become artists to work like assembly lines.

Tucker frequently runs into this same hitch in the game: It just doesn't add up. There's a trace of mystery. He's not going to out-right *ask*, of course. That would be . . . simply forbidden. "I don't know how much any of my friends make. Not a single one. I'm curious. I'm *really* curious, in a couple of cases," he says. "But I can't ask. I want to avoid the topic so much in my own life, I don't want to raise it in anyone else's."

Yet he thinks he has found the key that fits the lockbox of all of these situations. When the money that must be coming in isn't cov-ering the money that must be going out, there's money behind the scenes.

They have family money.

They have trust funds.

They have rich wives.

He knows something is going on that he can't see. Money is being injected from somewhere.

One way he knows this is because that's the secret in his own household. In more ways than one.

The house, as explained, was given to them outright. His in-laws also paid the children's school tuition bills, including college. Other-wise, the kids would have gone to public school and taken student loans for college. Also, although they have never used any of it to live on, his wife has accumulated a nest egg from her parents. Except for the house, that's their only asset, and they don't dip into it. If things get desperate, they could use it. It will probably have to be used in their retirement, if that stage in their lives ever actually hap-pens, which to them seems doubtful. *How far would it go? I mean, just how large is this nest egg?*

Tucker pauses.

"That's a very good question," he says.

He actually doesn't know.

"It's really her business," he says. He *could* figure it out, roughly, from their taxes—except she does the taxes and he doesn't examine them. Or he could look at a statement. Or he could simply ask her, after more than twenty-five years of marriage, about their nest egg.

It's not that she doesn't want him to know. In fact, she wonders why he doesn't find out about the money. It comes out in arguments, when she says in exasperation, *You don't even know how much money I have in the bank!*

Like with the finances of his neighbors and friends, he speculates. He can roughly piece it together. He has a guesstimate.

I would have thought that as one gets older, the money taboo would fade. I thought that with maturity would come, well, maturity: that we would only grow more self-confident, that we would have a lower tolerance for bull, and that at last money would lose its grip on our psyche.

But not so. In fact, the taboo gets stronger.

Let's note first that money as a basis of comparison and a measure of self-worth is generally more important to men than to women, according to psychologists and financial advisers. So we'll address what is basically the male mentality.

Here's what is at work: We expect that once we're all grown up and have a career behind us, we'll finally be settled, financially and emotionally. The crossing-over point seems to be around age fifty. That's when the gentlemen start to come into the role of patriarch. Their parents are fading, and they're next in line to be in charge. They're not the kids anymore, and if they still need help, they're going to have to figure it out themselves. Scary.

The last thing anybody wants to face down is that they're not ready to be in charge, that they're financially unprepared, that they're not where they think they should be, and time is running out. Once you've reached full maturity, drawing that line at around fifty, having financial stress is personally and socially unacceptable. It feels shameful.

So the clam tightens.

Sociologist Erving Goffman noted that "embarrassment has to do with unfulfilled expectations." He was talking about personal encounters, but that's also true in a general social context. We become, consciously or subconsciously, skilled at deception. "Whatever his position in society," Goffman wrote, "the person insulates himself by blindness, half-truths, illusions and rationalizations." That pretty much covers what's going on at this stage with a large swath of the boomers. Because they are not financially secure, they feel threatened. They're anxious, and they're hiding it.

Hiding the anxiety only makes it worse, for the individual and for everyone else. The more we suffer alone, the more we suffer. "Anxiety is not obvious in the way depression is obvious," says psychologist Scott Wetzler. "It's more of a personal, internal experience. You can hide it, and most people *do*. Don't let that fool you into thinking others aren't also anxious."

That's what we do, though. We go by appearances: *Others seem to be doing fine, so they must be doing fine.* We, by comparison, then become self-diagnosed failures. "In this age of soaring expectations, life is inevitably full of personal failures," writes psychologist Martin Seligman. He is trying to explain why the baby boomers, even nearly twenty years ago, had higher rates of depression than any other age group. Although one might guess that the highest rate of suicide is among young people, actually the highest rate is among those age sixty-five and older. With their history of depression combined with real or perceived financial woes, the boomers, as they get old, seem poised to have an even bigger problem with that than others have had.

The better you feel you should have done, the more difficult the letdown. If you're a college graduate headed for your twenty-fifth reunion, the expectations are high. They're high at every reunion, but the twenty-fifth, after a goodly chunk of your career, marks a special point of dead reckoning: where are you expected to be versus where have you gotten. That's what the college-educated boomers are in the midst of right now: attending, or avoiding, their twenty-fifth reunions.

One response for self-defined underperformers is simply not to show up. As writer Daphne Merkin puts it, "The problem with college reunions—I know this without having attended any—is that they leave room for too much soul-scorching realism . . . When it comes to one's peers it's not hard to find oneself at either pole of envy or smugness." The first thing to realize about reunion gatherings is this: Those most susceptible to envy are more likely to stay home, while the smug can't wait to get there. It's Class Notes on cocktails.

Take the example of one of the toughest crowds out there: the twenty-fifth reunion of the Harvard Class of 1977. "There's the usual Harvardian raft of venture capitalists, retired boy wonder tech starter-uppers, chiefs of surgery and lawyers of every stripe," class member Bo Emerson, a journalist, describes it. According to a class survey, the median income for the men was $200,000. (Bill Gates would have pushed it up a notch—and exploded the average—but he dropped out before graduation.) "Everyone at the reunion had some anxiety and trepidation, and most of us had some sleepless nights over it," says psychologist Scott Wetzler, himself a member of the class. He led a group discussion at the reunion on "Aspirations, Then and Now." Once the discussion got rolling, classmates talked about how they had disappointed themselves, with a common complaint being that they hadn't made enough money. It didn't matter how well they had actually done—some had made millions and still felt let down; it was all about comparisons to others, and about what they expected of themselves. But they also realize it's not okay to discuss these hangups. "We'll never complain about this out loud, out in the real world," Emerson says. "It's like complaining about the lack of well-trained butlers. Nobody wants to know about the painful expectations weighing on overprivileged Harvard grads."

Except maybe we do want to know about it, because the rest of us, while we assume at least the Harvard gang must be doing fine, are also wrestling with living up to expectations. Getting through life has become as big a head game as getting through the night.

Payday is coming. And not in a good way.

The boomer fantasy—that anything is possible, that money is something tangential—for Tucker is pretty much gone. "Money is the thing that colors everything. It's the underlying reality of everything," he says. "I'd rather think about other things, but it's something that's not going to take care of itself."

For him that means forgetting a green vista of retirement. Possibly forgetting retirement altogether. Certainly forgetting what some others his age are starting to talk about: winding down, stopping the daily grind, maybe retreating to a second home half of the year.

"I can't even think in those terms," Tucker says. "I'm still trying to figure out what I'm doing next. There are realities that are now hitting home. I never lived my life for a pension—so I have to deal with that now."

He is facing the reality that after age fifty there are more working years behind him than ahead. Tucker sits down every day to work and asks himself consciously, *Is this how I should be spending my time?*

Every minute now has become precious. Tucker has had to let go of a key notion his generation was raised with: the sense of limitlessness. The feelings that he could do *this*, or *that*, or *write that novel!* have been replaced with cold assessments about what is really possible, and how deep the sacrifices can go.

At this age, Tucker feels the tug of three generations at once. He has himself and his wife to think about, and their security and comfort as they approach retirement age. That's why he went to work for a regular paycheck when they were first married, and that's why he's still taking on assignments in his midfifties.

He still worries if his three children, who are still students, will have everything they need. "It's an issue," he says. "What if they try to live like me? I don't have anything to help out and make their lives easier."

And there are his parents. They're in their mideighties now and getting frail. They haven't planned for the expense of long-term care, should they need it. "It's not a pretty thing," Tucker says. "I can't help them. It's going to be rough. I've got my fingers crossed." Depending on what happens and what the expenses are, Tucker has thought about having to dive back into the proper working world. After all this time of somehow juggling to make his life work, he could end up in a job he doesn't want so that he can support his parents. "We have to come to grips with the practical realities," he says of the boomers. "The only way around it is to have *serious* money. That's something I never expected, and others didn't either."

As with many of the baby boomers, Tucker's major asset is his house. He and his wife could live off the money from selling it—assuming the real estate market holds until they would sell it, which is a risky assumption—but they would have to downsize and live in a far less expensive area. Preferably someplace that provides health-care beyond Medicare. Tucker has visited these places, he has heard about their advantages: incentives for retirees, tax-free zones, discounted medical care, and cheap property, with views. Others like him have already gone: to Mexico, Costa Rica, Panama, Belize. These places have marketed to American retirees. With a sort of Statue-of-Liberty style pitch, they say, *Come* here, *even with a modest income. You'll live well, we'll take care of you. We want you.*

It could be a final tradeoff: leave the country altogether and move to Central or South America.

"Is it time to cash out and do things differently?" Tucker wonders. "I'm thinking hard about cutting and running."

CHAPTER SIX

෨

Behind the Hedges

When I told my sister I was going to Palm Beach for an interview, she advised me to drive around the nice neighborhood by the ocean.

"That's where the gorgeous homes are," she told me, then added with disappointment, "not that you can see much, since they all have high hedges."

I didn't tell her that I expected to see plenty, that my interview was going to be *behind* the hedges.

I was, to be honest, slightly nervous. When I had arranged the interview with an assistant, I had been invited to stay. I wasn't sure what to expect. Would I be dealing with staff? Would my sources appear for the interview and then disappear for the rest of the day? What would I do the rest of the time? Or were they just like any family? Maybe we would curl up in the family room and watch a video after dinner?

My flight was delayed and I had to call the residence to tell them. I thought about calling the assistant instead—they seemed to like everything filtered through the assistant—but then thought, *That's silly. Just call.* The wife, Middy, answered the phone herself, even though it took me a while to realize it was her. She thanked me profusely for letting her know about the delayed flight and said she would be picking me up herself. She described her car for me: a blue *something*. Oh no, I thought, I'm terrible at recognizing cars. Since we live in New York City, I drive once or twice a year at most and my sisters laugh at me when I describe a rental car as "um, an SUV?"

"What kind of car is it again?" I asked Middy, hoping to understand the general shape of the thing.

"A big blue convertible."

Ah-ha! Now she was speaking my language.

I recognized her, all right. No problem. As I gazed along a line of cars creeping along the airport's pickup lane, an enormous convertible came whipping over from the fast lane. I would have described it as some sort of supersized Mercedes—I didn't know they even made them that big. Middy had one hand loosely on the reins of the car and was vigorously waving the other one overhead, bursting with enthusiasm at the sight of a visitor, even though I was almost a complete stranger to her. Her little white dog was hopping around on her lap. I tossed my bag in the backseat and we sped off toward the ocean.

When the gates opened to their property, we drove in beneath the palms, took a turn, and Middy announced, "We'll drop you at your house first, so you can get settled."

"Wow," I said as we pulled up alongside gardens and a golf-green–clipped lawn, leading to a large villa. "This is beautiful!"

As we got out of the car, knowing I would be impressed with the property, Middy said outright, "You want to write about money? Now you can see money." The car, which she had to point out to me was a Bentley, was meant as an appetizer.

"Yeah," I said, "but you're supposed to be telling me about the downside."

She froze for a full second, then recovered her congeniality. "I'll tell you that too," she promised.

And she kept her word.

There's something about Middy. At baseline, she's a free spirit. She can kind of suck you in with her energy and openheartedness. She has a definite irreverence for formality or even convention. Even when she barely knows you, she's interested in you. She's a hugger and a toucher, much like her terrier, who can't tell the famous guests from the plebeians, and wouldn't care anyway, so leaps up to lick both in the face.

She's in her fifties and doesn't try to disguise a day of it. She wears her gray and white hair naturally, no fussing. She gets ready to go out in a few minutes, whether it's for a walk on the beach or a black-tie dinner. Her body is strong—not molded-by-a-personal-trainer strong, but morning yoga and lots-of-time-in-nature strong.

Middy is no actor. When you say something she thinks is incorrect or incomprehensible, she won't smile politely or just give a hint of disagreement. "What?!" she'll say suddenly, and furrow her brow, and you almost want to apologize right then rather than explain yourself.

Her husband explained, "She doesn't care who anyone is!" in a way that said that he himself does care, quite a bit, who's who. Yet he meant it, I think, with both some embarrassment and some pride. Once they were at an international party and she danced a lot with an older gentleman. After the event, Middy's husband asked what she'd thought of the prince.

Who? she asked him. *I didn't meet any prince.*

When she was told she'd been dancing with him half the night, she snuffed, *He's a prince? I just saw some old fart sitting there and thought he could use some dancing!*

When Middy and her husband were sitting around at the weekend residence of the American president, the president was excitedly explaining the painting that hung over the mantel and described how much it changed when one looked at it close up. He told Middy to go look more closely and see what he meant. To the distress of her husband, she didn't budge from her seat and flatly told the president, *No. I'm comfortable right here.*

At first it all seems to fit: When you're one of the wealthiest people on the planet, you don't have to impress anyone. *Of course you're carefree!* I thought. *What a feeling it would be to have all of that money, to be able to go anywhere you want to and do anything and meet anyone and have anything you desire.*

Except it's not like that. That became clear even after two days in Palm Beach. Despite our fantasies, money cannot change your life that much—it can't change who you are, and it certainly can't take away your problems.

Middy sometimes seems like a sunflower that sprouted up in the middle of a formal garden. And it's the sunflower that makes the cultivated roses look like they are the ones out of place. But then, when you know her better, you find out that it's a struggle for the sunflower, just like for the roses and for everyone else.

A year before she met her husband—I call him Citizen Q—Middy had prayed for his arrival. She was on a retreat with Native Americans. It was July, and she and her boyfriend—a monk with no worldly possessions except his frock—had come out west on a hiking trip and were taking part in the Sun Dance ceremony. The men in the group spend three days in a ritual circle, fasting, chanting, dancing and drumming. Staying outside the circle, the women support them with prayers.

Middy was supposed to distance herself from the rest of the community because she had her period. Native Americans think of the "moon cycle" as a time of reflection and renewal for a woman.

So she carried her tent—in that case it's called a "moon hut"—away from the main camp and set it up along the river where she could be alone with nature. Listening to the drumming in the distance, Middy stripped off her clothes and slipped into the river. She floated on her back and felt the warm air and the cold water, which cleared her mind. When she climbed out of the water, she sat on a soft patch of green moss along the edge of the river and, as the Natives had taught her, let the blood flow back into the earth. She felt completely serene and connected with the world. She looked up into the sky, and at that moment she made some decisions, and some requests.

First, she'd had it with the monk. She had thought that money and material comforts made no difference to her. She had grown up in a well-off family, but money had been used to manipulate: Gifts were given with conditions or sometimes retracted, promises were made and often broken, she was alternately spoiled and denied. So sometimes she had money, sometimes she didn't, and she trained herself not to care, not to desire a material lifestyle. She didn't depend on it for her happiness. Middy is generous and a caretaker by nature, but on the moss she realized she didn't want always to be the one to support everyone else. It was tough enough being a single mother and responsible for making all of the decisions about her daughter's upbringing—she didn't want to be financially responsible for another adult too.

She was ready, she decided, for another man to come into her life. She wanted to find a partner, in all senses. And she asked, quite specifically, for him: *Let it be somebody who accepts me for who I am. Somebody older. And let it be somebody with money.*

After the hiking trip, Middy broke up with the monk and waited for her accepting, older man of means. Months passed. In the meantime, she kept busy with her work.

One day the next summer, someone handed Middy a tape at

work and asked her to play it. When she put it on, to her surprise she was surrounded by a familiar sound: Native American drumming. Her mind went straight back to the moments by the river out west the previous summer. *Ah-ha*, she thought with a smile.

Native Americans believe that prayers are answered one year later. She had recently met someone, and now she realized he was the one she had wished for.

She had to laugh, as she hiked through woods one afternoon thinking about her good fortune. All of her requests had been granted. The man she started dating was sensitive and accepting of her, just as she had wanted. He was indeed more mature. And as for the money . . .

I never meant to ask for someone with that *much money!* Middy told the trees as she hiked. *I just wanted someone with an income, maybe $100,000 a year. You can live quite well on that.*

Citizen Q was high on the list of the wealthiest people in the country. A billionaire.

At first it was pretty neat, of course. Middy and her daughter flew to New York City for the daughter's birthday, and Citizen Q had them over to his Fifth Avenue apartment for dinner. When they were driven back to their hotel in a limousine, they giggled at the fun of it.

For a change, rather than her always taking care of everyone else, someone was taking care of Middy. Citizen Q was an old-fashioned suitor who gave little gifts and called her every day. When she went to his farmhouse for dinner dates, she was wowed by the romance of a table brimming with fresh flowers and glowing with candlelight.

And yet, something was just slightly amiss. The romantic dinners for two were a little . . . crowded. As they talked and ate, the dining-room door flip-flapped, and other faces kept appearing. Their conversations wound into many different ears.

Citizen Q was used to it, and it didn't bother him at all that as they leaned in to each other, someone else was there filling their water glasses. Some of the time Middy thought it was a treat to be waited on. Other times, she couldn't wait to escape to the garden so they could walk hand in hand and sit together on a bench with some privacy.

One solution, a way to get away from the formal staff for an evening, was for Middy to have Citizen Q over to her place for dinner. It was more cozy there, and she would cook for him.

On the first attempt, Citizen Q came rolling up to the house in an unusual, brushed-metal sports car. When Middy came out to greet him, however, she saw that he hadn't come alone. He wasn't driving the sports car but riding in it. Middy tried to ignore this anomaly.

On the second such date, Citizen Q was chauffeured to her door on the wrong side of a sleek black Corvette. He was trying to show off his fleet of exotic cars, but she wasn't impressed. This time Middy told him how silly it was. The next time he came over, he managed to pilot a Land Rover on his own.

Just as she was more comfortable hosting him in her own quarters, he was more comfortable being waited on by hired help. He didn't want Middy to have to trouble herself with tasks like cooking. He had worked very hard amassing his fortune, and he enjoyed being able to delegate. He wanted to give that to Middy too, for her to be waited on in style.

They were back at his house for dinner. Middy wanted to make him as comfortable as he was trying to make her. But then . . .

Ding-ding! ding-ding!

Citizen Q was calling the help by ringing his little silver bell. Middy found it ridiculous.

You live like a king! she announced to him. *This is like royalty!*

She meant it as an observation more than a criticism, but to her surprise he took great offense.

What do you mean?! he erupted. *I do not!*

Citizen Q might have been as rich as a king, but he didn't think of himself that way. Perhaps because a few other people in the world really do live in palaces with official entourages. It's not about where we are but how we see ourselves.

Let's try to figure out the specifics of wealth. How much is enough? How much is "rich"?

The pitfall: The second you set out striving to get to a number and thinking that much will bring security and contentment, you've just put yourself in orbit to nowheresville. There's no there there. It's like trying to get to a parking spot at the horizon.

When I was in journalism school I talked to an alum who had written a lot of freelance articles for what was my favorite newspaper. He told me he wasn't writing for them much anymore, though, despite the prestige of the publication, because they didn't pay well enough. When I asked how much they paid, he said around $250.

Two hundred and fifty dollars?! I thought to myself. *Great!*

Before grad school I had been writing articles for a free weekly newspaper for $35 (and bartending on the side). So $250—half a month's rent at the time—seemed generous. You know what's coming, though. Soon I was writing articles for $400, $750, and then over $1,000, and I, too, had to cut back on my favorite publication because I felt I couldn't afford it anymore.

Did I just need to earn enough to live on? Yes and no. How much do any of us really need to live on? That's the Great Moving Target.

When I was at dinner with Middy and Citizen Q, he was talking about the high cost of living in New York City—a topic I am intimately familiar with. Except his version of you-can't-scrape-by-even-on-this-amount was quite different than mine.

"Apartments are so expensive. School tuition, child care, parking . . . even the groceries cost a lot," he lamented while I nodded in agreement. Then he announced, "Even on $500,000 a year, you're nowhere." I stopped midnod.

Nowhere?

The fact is, there are 8 million people living in New York City. Of those, an estimated 30,000 make more than $500,000. The rest of us, I'd say, are not *nowhere*, but right here.

But okay, we're off to the races with The Number.

For many years, the common notion of big-time income success was breaking six figures: $100,000. The *New York Times* recently ran an article formally announcing that $100,000 didn't mean much anymore, and that $200,000 is the new $100,000.

Yet, even going back to the late 1980s, the same newspaper trumpeted that "investment bankers under 30 with staggering $600,000-a-year incomes are not rich and may never be." That was two decades ago, which means that, at least in the bubble of New York, we're at a $1 million income threshold to be, as Citizen Q might put it, somewhere. A recent magazine cover story confirmed that figure (it's unclear with what degree of sarcasm) as the minimum needed for living well these days.

I interviewed the young owner of an advertising business once who thought he hadn't been making nearly enough money. His business was grossing $2 million with few employees and was very profitable, so much of that money was going into his pocket. The trouble, as he put it, was that his friends whom he met through the Young Entrepreneurs Organization were already buying summer houses and taking Fridays off. Even though he made an extraordinary amount of money compared to the vast majority of people, in the small subset of peers he compared himself to, he wasn't keeping up. At best, he was irked. At worst, he felt like a failure.

Maybe assets are what matter, not how much you make but how much you have in the storehouse. Not long ago, $1 million was viewed as more money than one could possibly need over a lifetime. Does $1 million now make a person wealthy, let alone set for life? It should, since only about 1 in 100 Americans ever accumulates that kind of money. We live on misperceptions, however. Ask those who do have $1 million just how much it is, and for many it doesn't seem like a whole lot, either because they're planning to get much more, or because they've settled on a lifestyle that even $1 million in assets cannot support.

Who's really wealthy, then? Who's not worrying? Who has *arrived*? The figure of $10 million has been floated in recent years as a solid target. Owning $10 million in assets (*liquid* assets) will get you into the private banking category at some banks and brokerage houses. It will not, however, mean you are entitled to their top-tier service. There are still plenty of wealthier people above you. The ultrahigh net worth categories start at $20 million or even $100 million.

One hundred million dollars. Enough? Not enough to get on the *Forbes* 400 list of wealthiest Americans. You currently need $750 million to dangle from the lowest rung there. And don't you think, once you were in that club, that you would gun for the big time, for $1 billion? (I mean, not *you*, of course. You yourself would never think $750 million wasn't plenty. It's the other people with the problem. It's always the other people.) And for the about 300 billionaires in the country who have made it there, is *that* enough? *Forbes* ran an article accompanying the annual list titled "Billionaire Blues," which led off with the statement, "Contrary to the popular myth, if you suddenly woke up and found that you had inherited $1 billion, you could not simply live off the interest on your fortune." They were referring to the pressure to live like other billionaires do, which means having at least a couple of well-placed residences, a private jet, a "proper" art collection, and certainly a yacht, with a year-round crew. Even billionaires must, after all, keep up with their Joneses.

The wealthy do still keep up with the Joneses. Oh yes. Like anyone, they are constantly confronted by people who have more. Not every one of them is materialistic and craves attention; as with the rest of the population, some are like that and some are not. For fun, let's look at the ones who are.

A story in the *Wall Street Journal* recently described turmoil in the world of yachts. Owning a yacht, and maintaining it and its staff all year round for the handful of times you'll actually use it, has for a number of years served as a status symbol that you're rich enough, for practical purposes, not to be counting your money anymore. The vessels can cost tens of millions of dollars to build and easily over $1 million a year to maintain. In that circle, a 100-foot yacht used to be quite impressive. A businessman who owns one that size said he used to consider it "a good-sized boat." Then a 130-footer pulled up next to him at a boat show in Florida, and his pride shriveled. Compared to the other boats, he complained, "Now it's like a dinghy."

You're not special now if your boat doesn't stretch a solid 200 feet. A few years ago, the CEO of Limited built a 315-footer that he named, optimistically, Limitless. It wasn't. Microsoft co-founder Paul Allen acquired a 354-footer. He then put in an order for what was to be the world's largest yacht, the *Octopus*, at 414 feet. At that time, the CEO of Oracle had his own craft under construction, named *Rising Sun*, that was initially to run 393 feet. As the *Octopus* stretched, however, so did *Rising Sun*. Measuring in at a final 452 feet, *Rising Sun* reigned as the world's biggest bath toy. For a moment. In the world's yacht battle, it's high noon again. In the spring of 2005 a prince in the United Arab Emirates floated a 525-footer.

Even at amounts of wealth that only the slimmest sliver of the world's population ever achieve, a pecking order emerges. Just as on any school playground, in any suburban neighborhood, comparisons are made. Inferiority is felt.

A journalist went on a mission in Manhattan to figure out who those people are who hang out in ritzy cafes on workday afternoons. At a chic cafe in SoHo, she talked to an expensively dressed twenty-four-year-old artist. He had dropped out of college after studying photography and now wasn't employed, to the chagrin of his family. He was spending the afternoon drinking multiple lemonades with two friends. Still, the young man professed, he isn't rich. Not like some people he knows. "Like the *Born Rich* movie," he said. "That's an entirely different ballgame. I'm the poorest kid of the rich kids."

What about the *Born Rich* kids, then? Those are the wealthy friends of Jamie Johnson whom he interviewed for his documentary about growing up with extreme wealth. Is it, indeed, a different game? Maybe their families do have more money, but the comparison and ranking continue. Although the sense of competition and keeping up is not discussed in the film, Johnson talks about it on the side, in interviews and in the director's commentary. He confesses that the day he was filming Donald Trump's daughter Ivanka in her girlhood bedroom on the 68th floor of Trump Tower, he was distracted by the view out the window, because he'd "never been to an apartment like that in New York until that day." Although to the unknowing eye, all of the characters in the film seem like they're in the same category—ultrawealthy—and their family fortunes are indeed among the biggest in the world, Johnson makes it clear that there are, to them, noticeable differences.

In the 1940s, anthropologist Margaret Mead distinguished the "upper upper" class member in America as "someone whose only possible social movement is downward." Even in Johnson's league, there's still room for upward mobility. So by Mead's standard, Johnson isn't a member of the upper upper class, even though it sure seems like it to the rest of us.

Citizen Q and Middy's first outing as a couple was a high-society fundraiser at the Waldorf in New York. They got dressed in black tie and evening gown and were driven to the hotel. Going to society events was a big part of Citizen Q's life, and when they walked in, Middy saw why. People crowded around and fell over him. Lots of photos were taken.

Nobody recognized her, and Citizen Q didn't introduce her. She got brushed aside. It was the school lunchroom dynamic all over again. Middy, even though she has a genuinely amiable, outgoing personality, retreated to a corner of the room and sat there alone. It was the first of many such evenings when that would happen. Citizen Q would get swept up in a tide of guests and hosts, and Middy would drift off by herself. She even learned to bring a book with her. "Sitting in the corner isn't so bad," she says. "You observe."

What she observed was that the room was full of two hundred or more guests, but they weren't mingling. Everyone there was wealthy, or they wouldn't have been invited. But Middy saw the guests stratify right before her. What mattered was *how* wealthy you were, how important, how famous. A pecking order emerged within what was already a top layer of society's pecking order. Middy was an unknown. An outsider. "People never knew I had a wealthy background," she says. "There I was, this poor little rich girl."

As soon as they got into the car at the end of that first evening, Middy turned to Citizen Q with annoyance.

You should have gone alone! she told him.

He didn't know what she was talking about. He thought they had both had a grand time.

It certainly hadn't been her scene. She not only didn't fit in, she didn't want to. People did have a lot of reasons to like Citizen Q for himself—he's a fun and giving person—but there wasn't much excuse for the fawning over him, except that he was fabulously wealthy. She saw the black-tie world as an illusion. "The life goal is money, and you have money, so they come to you," Middy explains. "You're treated differently before they know who you are. They aren't at all interested in you."

When they got home from the event, Middy showed her repulsion for the world of illusion by bowing down to Citizen Q and saying, *You're god, you're god.*

They had some negotiating to do. For Citizen Q, the reward for having been so successful financially was to indulge in high style and luxury. He bought a string of Bentleys and gave one to Middy. She liked the comfort and ease of having wealth, and she appreciated things like being able to buy beautiful art. She enjoyed the access to the interesting people who congregate around the wealthy.

"Most people think this lifestyle is very desirable," she says. And yet that's part of the pressure of it—that it is *supposed* to be so desirable, so wonderful, but there is a side to it that can be confining and uncomfortable. When she was dating Citizen Q, a friend asked her earnestly, *How is it making love with a billionaire?* She had to report, *It's the same as with anyone else.* Then she commented later, "Isn't it funny how we imagine there's something different?"

There are, of course, differences in the trappings of life, if not the life functions themselves. Citizen Q ran the household like a business, and scores of people were on the payroll. Gardeners alone numbered in the dozens. There was always somebody hovering. Yes, they were doing their jobs and trying to please Citizen Q and Middy—but there was also the constant lack of privacy that had initially bothered Middy. And there was intrigue. They found out that one servant used to listen at the door to their conversations and had been writing everything down in a little black book. (They had to burn it.)

Middy wasn't in favor of large household staffs and multiple residences. She didn't find it necessary or comfortable, and she explained this to Q. Wouldn't one house and three or four people to help out be more than enough? At first he agreed, and the staff was trimmed back dramatically. But soon Citizen Q acquired one European residence for them, then another, then another. He couldn't do it, he told her. He loved luxury. This was how people with copious amounts of wealth could live, this is how the rest of his class *did* live—and he wanted to, too.

Citizen Q bought an extensive set of fine china from an auction house. It arrived in crates, and as the butler was unpacking and unwrapping the plates, he kept *ooh*-ing and *ahh*-ing over them, telling Middy how impressive they were. When she didn't show much interest in the stack of new dishes, he asked with some incredulity, *Aren't you excited?*

No, she explained flatly. *I'm not excited. These are just dishes. I wouldn't know anything more precious than a child and a relationship.*

Sometimes, over the years of being with Citizen Q, Middy felt like she was losing her own identity. The fakeness of the society circles still got to her. People so clearly treated her differently because she was Mrs. Q. Sometimes when she was entertaining at their home, guests who didn't know who she was wouldn't reciprocate any interest in talking to her. Then she watched their embarrassed reactions when they realized she was the hostess. To her it shouldn't have mattered, but to them it did.

Then there was the yacht incident. Citizen Q owned a yacht that rivaled the best of them. Specially built for him in Europe, it came with its own crew and a large staff that, as Middy described it, just like at home would take care of everything for you except going to the bathroom (although, of course, they would run the bathwater). On one vacation, Middy's young daughter brought along her closest friend from school. The friend, Lucy, lived in a mobile home. The couple and the girls flew in a private plane down to the Caribbean. From the boat they scuba-dived, and on board they were cooked for and waited on. One morning, Citizen Q announced irritably to Middy, *Lucy can't come with us on the boat again.*

Why? Middy asked, not able to imagine why Q would say that, as Lucy was a sweet girl and a great friend to Middy's daughter.

She's rude, Citizen Q explained with exasperation. *She never says "good morning" to me!*

Middy exploded. She banged her hand down hard on the table and yelled at Q. *Do you have any idea what it's like for her?* she asked him. *Do you have any idea how intimidating all of this is to her? How intimidating* you *are? What if, just once, the Great Mr. Q would go over to Lucy and say "good morning" to* her*?!*

He looked at her silently, then tears came to his eyes. One overflowed down his cheek.

I never thought about it like that, he said.

Perceptions and misperceptions are a big problem in the world of the wealthy. Having an abundance of money can cause as many problems as having little of it. It's easy for us to cluck at that notion: *Oh, like what?!* Yet that reaction is a big part of the problem. While we say we know that money doesn't bring happiness, not so deep down we still believe it does.

Why, after all, are we so fascinated by the wealthy? We watch guided tours of their houses on TV, gawk at photos of their designer dresses, read about what they ate at a restaurant only they and theirs could get into, and want to see the hotel suite they stayed in on vacation. We imagine ourselves, for a moment, in their lives. With so much money, with so many toys, so many options, so much attention and assistance, so much luxury and glamour, their lives must be so exciting, so comfortable, so . . . happy! And when we discover any fault, see them caught frowning, hear of an argument, read of their troubles of any kind, we don't have the same sympathy we would normally have for anyone else, anyone more like us. We eat it up. We *want* them to have problems, we want to scoff. After all, they're just being petty and childish, we think. Their problems aren't *real*, like ours. The rest of us are genuinely struggling here, whereas they bring their nonsense on themselves. Don't they? They have no right to complain.

The rich, those with millions of dollars, let's say, are on to this. They can guess how we think of them, and they know we're not going to understand how they can have genuine problems. They've very well picked up on the idea that if you've got lots of money to spend and are living in a big house with lots of very expensive accoutrements, your life must be *fabulous!* Just like VH1 says it is.

The message is so strong that the rich are to be envied, that the wealthy themselves start to believe the myth. They themselves believe that their lives really should be better because they have so much wealth. When, as a wealthy person, your life does not seem so fabulous—because it is true that money *doesn't* buy happiness—it's that much more confusing, disappointing, and lonely.

To whom do you turn, then? With whom can you come clean, when you're rich but unhappy? Not very many people.

In all classes, money has been shepherded into its own special chamber of preoccupation and mystery. The taboo against discussing money, and any troubles it sprouts, is especially strong within the upper class. Children who grow up in wealthy families often either hear nothing on the subject, or they are given stern instructions not to discuss it. Either scenario leads them to see money as a secret, and having lots of it as something bad, something shameful. The grown-up version is to treat money, and especially its effects, as an intensely private matter. Even painfully private.

There's a big disconnect there to contend with: Society says you should be very happy if you have a lot of money. So when you do have a lot of money and are still not happy, you along with everyone else can start to wonder why. But you don't want to reveal the problems you're inevitably having, despite being wealthy, because then you'll feel the sting of criticism. You end up feeling pressured to live up to the societal expectations. Jessie O'Neill, granddaughter of a president of General Motors who inherited a fortune in her twenties, said, "Let's face it, we are seldom all that we appear to be, and the more glittering and attractive the external package, the greater the inner sense of dishonesty a person might feel for not living up to a larger-than-life image."

The wealthy are often even prevented from getting professional help from a therapist or an adviser. The first reason is a concern that nobody will sympathize. Therapists, even though they're trained to be professional, are still human, and most of them are not multimillionaires, which puts wealthy patients in the uncomfortable position of discussing money problems with someone who has much less than they do. And they're right that thoughts of ridicule do sometimes go through a therapist's mind. A therapist in Manhattan had a man come in depressed over losing $34 million in the stock market. He was in despair because he was poor now, he told the therapist. She got right down to work with him. Then it came out that he wasn't exactly *poor*, that he still had *some* money left, he said.

How much? the therapist asked him outright.

After some reluctance, he told her: *Fifteen million.*

When the therapist told me this story, she paused after the revelation of the $15 million and raised her eyebrows in silence. Her message was clear.

Another woman explained to the therapist that she could not afford to pay the full fee. Sympathetic, the therapist accepted a reduced rate, and their sessions went on for several months. Then one day the woman revealed that her income was $400,000. It wasn't that she couldn't afford the therapist's bill, she just felt like she didn't have enough. At times like that it becomes clear to both patient and therapist that they have different perspectives on the world.

A handful of super-wealthy people have themselves become therapists and set up practices designed specifically for clients like themselves. They start off with a personal understanding of the dynamics of wealth and can therefore set their patients more at ease from the beginning. The patients know they are less likely to be judged and more likely to find some sympathy when they are dealing with someone from their world. Because of the strong demand, some of these therapists have developed a booming niche business.

The second reason that members of the upper class can be reluctant to seek counseling is concern for privacy. Many of us are not comfortable with the idea of a stranger hearing our deepest problems and secrets, and that feeling is compounded when the therapist is likely to recognize your name and "who you are" when you come from a very wealthy family.

When Middy became increasingly confounded by her relationship with Citizen Q—they even bickered about money, like most couples—she tried to solve the problems by herself for maybe too long. On a couple of occasions she "left him" by packing her books and moving out—to the guest house. ("I realized I didn't have to move *out* to move out!" she says with some glee.) Friends eventually told her she should get help from a therapist. But the usual question arose: *Who?* She knew the therapists in town, did she want them hearing about their personal issues? And what would Citizen Q think of that?

The less that is revealed, the more dizzying the vicious circle of myth and secrecy about wealth becomes. The following poem is a powerful reminder that much goes on behind the scenes, even in the lives of those we envy, and that things are never as they seem:

Richard Cory

Whenever Richard Cory went down town,
We people on the pavement looked at him:
He was a gentleman from sole to crown,
Clean favored, and imperially slim.

He was always quietly arrayed,
And he was always human when he talked;
But still he fluttered pulses when he said,
"Good Morning," and he glittered when he walked.

And he was rich—yes, richer than a king—
And admirably schooled in every grace:
In fine, we thought that he was everything
To make us wish that we were in his place.

So on we worked, and waited for the light,
And went without the meat, and cursed the bread;
And Richard Cory, one calm summer night,
Went home and put a bullet through his head.

—Edwin A. Robinson (1869–1935)

In an anthology of best poems, the editors included this eerie footnote: "You can probably read an obituary for a Richard Cory in a local newspaper within the next twelve-month." In fact the poem, which later inspired the Simon and Garfunkel song of the same name, was derived from a newspaper story about a society man who committed suicide.

To my surprise, a couple of people I've shown the poem to said they didn't get it. *Why did the guy kill himself?* they asked. *What did I miss?*

That's exactly the point. How much we miss, and that we don't know what is really going on. Many readers of this poem are like the people on the pavement, seeing rich man Richard and maybe even feeling the envy. As the Simon and Garfunkel version goes, "He had everything a man could want: power, grace, style." What went wrong was that *we* were wrong. Richard was more miserable than any of us, yet all we saw were the "good things" in his life, and we wanted to be him without understanding him.

A wealthy woman, while growing up on the West Coast, watched the Richard Cory scenario unfold in her own life. Her father founded what is today an enormous corporation, and she and her siblings were raised amid great wealth, in what she calls "a beautiful, sheltered neighborhood." Even with the outward advantage of money, she had difficulty settling into a career, and she rushed into marriages that failed. Some among her peers were having an even harder time. One fatally overdosed on drugs. Another shot himself. By the time the woman was in her midthirties, there had been five suicides in that "sheltered" neighborhood. She realized, at last, that she hadn't been the only one struggling with such privilege. She went back to school for a degree in social work and started a psychotherapy practice centered on helping inheritors work through the emotional issues that, she says, are "kept under greater societal lock and key than in other populations."

One issue that Middy and Citizen Q wrestled with was how much to indulge their children. A self-made man, Citizen Q was eager for the children to make their own way in the world, just as he had. *I don't want them to get a free ride*, he would tell Middy. The problem was that not everyone else in their position was thinking that way. Some of the Joneses took delight in indulging their own children. Then the adult children of different families ended up comparing themselves: Who had more help? Who was living more luxuriously?

One of their children in particular, Katie, as a young adult had an issue with how much support she was receiving from her family. Her friend's parents had given her friend a house: How come Katie wasn't given a house too? She watched Citizen Q giving millions away to nonprofits, and she accused him of taking care of everyone else before he took care of his own children. "There's a societal expectation," Middy says. "You can give your kids cars and a house, et cetera, and it's done by some, so there's an expectation for you to do it too."

Eventually they gave in and gave Katie a property. She sold it. Then she asked them for more money. They gave her another property. The more they gave her, the more kept . . . *disappearing*.

"We knew something was going on," Middy says.

They figured out what it was when one of their younger children came back from one of Katie's parties and talked about the guests having white powder on their noses.

Then it was time for sure to call in professional help. But again the important question was, *Who?* Normally they would rely on their financial adviser or lawyer for advice on how to handle money matters. But that wasn't personal enough for this kind of issue. They needed, as my husband and I had needed, someone knowledgeable about money issues who was also part psychologist, part confessor, and part fixer. Just as I had done when I had been bewildered, Middy turned to the Internet in search of some sort of money doctor.

She had better luck finding one than I had. Working with the superwealthy is a closet niche but a profitable one. So Middy was able to tap into the small, semi-underground group of experts trained to handle the touchy issues that surround having lots of money.

Some of the problems could be solved outside of the money doctors' offices if the wealthy were talking with one another. The taboo is real, though, so just like the rest of us, wealthy people too often wrestle with thinking it's only them. "There is generally great family pressure in the upper class to maintain that external appearance of perfection, never admitting that there is a problem in paradise," writes Jessie O'Neill in her book *The Golden Ghetto: The Psychology of Affluence.*

One issue that lurks—on a more basic level than problems like substance addiction, which we do hear something about—is guilt over good fortune. Despite what the rest of us think it would be like to have enormous wealth, it comes with carryons—too many for the overhead bin. Wealth guilt can strike anyone who realizes they are more fortunate than most people and can't quite account for why. That means it's a special concern for those who didn't make their money on their own but rather inherited it. Just as those who endure misfortune wonder what they have done to deserve their lot, so too do those who have come into good fortune wonder the same thing. For them, the *Why me?* question can be especially perplexing. If we had to have one problem or the other, most of us would choose to do our wondering in luxurious surroundings. If wealth were weighing on our conscience, we figure we would just give some of our money away to prove ourselves worthy of the stewardship. However, that doesn't always lift the burden of guilt.

Psychologists have identified the discomfort we feel when we have much more or less than someone else and can't figure out why. They refer to it as equity theory. It means we value fairness and believe we should pretty much get what we deserve and deserve what we get, in comparison to others. We're upset if we perceive someone else is getting more than their share, but *we can also get upset if we perceive that we ourselves are getting more than we deserve.*

There was an experiment done in which a simulated company hired three sets of male secretaries for two weeks. One group was told they were getting paid more than the others, the second group was told they were getting paid less, and the third group was told that everyone was earning the same pay. In actuality, all of the workers were paid the same. However, the overpaid workers ended up being more productive and the underpaid workers were less productive. The workers naturally tried to even the score by living up to their wages. Most interesting, however, is that both the overpaid and the underpaid groups reported being less satisfied with their jobs than the group of workers who thought everyone was being paid the same.

The reason inheritors struggle with the unfairness issue more often than self-made millionaires is that the self-made people have an explanation for their good fortune: They earned it. The inheritors, on the other hand, were just born into it. Just as any of us can look at a wealthier person and think to ourselves, or have a gut reaction, that *that's not fair, something is not right here,* the person we're looking at can have a similar reaction. They sometimes *also* have the thought that *something is not right here.*

Fueling that notion are certain passages from the Bible that are often misconstrued to come across as a message that wealth is wrong. Ever hear that "money is the root of all evil"? The Scripture actually reads that "the love of money is a root of all kinds of evil" (1 Timothy 6:10). Big difference there. The same difference applies to the distinction between money and *mammon,* which one scholar defines as "money personified and deified." It's not having money that is against Jesus' teachings but rather the devotion to it, the worship of it.

What about it being "easier for a camel to pass through the eye of a needle, than for a rich man to enter the kingdom of God" (Matthew 19:24; Luke 18:25)? That's surely not a favorite biblical quotation for a lot of wealthy Christians. But again, it has been truncated so that its true meaning is often lost: Jesus added that "with God all things are possible."

In the parable that contains the camel and the eye of the needle passage, Jesus was talking to a wealthy man who was keeping the commandments and asked how he could do even better. When Jesus suggested he should sell all he owned and give it to the poor, the man couldn't bring himself to do it. "The man was a fool because he was a self-centered materialist who had forgotten God; he was not a fool because he had been a successful businessman," explains theology professor Ronald Nash. "Claims that the Bible condemns wealth or that God hates all the rich are clearly incompatible with the teachings of Jesus, who saw nothing inherently evil in money, wealth, or private ownership. While Jesus certainly condemned materialism and the compulsive quest for wealth, He never condemned wealth per se." In fact the Bible encourages both the creation and enjoyment of wealth.

Even though it would seem that being wealthy would make one feel very secure, many end up battling insecurity. Again, this is mostly an issue for inheritors versus those who are self-made. The self-made are generally not worried about losing their fortunes because they figure they did it once, they can do it all again. Inheritors, though, are unlikely to experience another windfall, and they often feel incapable of amassing wealth on their own. One inheritor summed up this mistaken philosophy of scarcity by saying "There's only so much, and when it's gone, it's gone." Another inheritor, who became a social worker in Massachusetts, pointed out, "Welfare people and inheritors have a lot in common. They both know they can't survive on their own."

Something else the wealthy wrestle with: Do people love me for *me*? It's what Middy encountered, being treated differently with extreme wealth on her side, and it made her feel distrustful of new "friends." She tells her friends who've known her a long time, *I'm so glad I knew you before I had money!* When one grows up with wealth, there can be little escaping its influence. People recognize your name, they know "who your family is," and under those circumstances the world works a little differently, which isn't always welcome. "It is not uncommon for a young inheritor to develop an intense desire to find out what life would be like without recognition as a 'rich person,'" writes Thayer Willis, an inheritor and therapist, in her book about coping with wealth's pitfalls.

Some inheritors go to great lengths to get away from the pressures of the upper class. Specifically, Willis describes a minimigration of the children of prominent East Coast families to the more relaxed Northwest, where they can live "normally." There, people don't know their names, and in some cases the inheritors change their names. They get jobs they know they got on their own merit, and they build a social circle of people who only know them for *them*. "No doubt it's scary, but it can also be thrilling to leave a world of security and privilege to enter a life of anonymity and challenge, where everything you receive is *earned* by you, not simply placed in your lap," Willis says. "There are two sides, you see, to a life of privilege."

In parts of the Northwest, to generalize, keeping up with the Joneses hinges more on who can live further *beneath* their means. Just as some people in more materialistic communities of the country are stretching beyond their means to keep up appearances of affluence, some people living in the Northwest who really *are* very wealthy are "slumming it," obscuring their money and striving to be on the same (lower) level as those around them. A friend of mine in Oregon was dating a guy for a while; they both worked for a living, and nothing seemed at all out of the ordinary. Then as they got more serious, he revealed he was sitting on a fortune. Again, things are not as they seem, and figuring out who people really are and what their lives are like becomes an expedition to the center of the onion.

Middy didn't stop working after she married Citizen Q. To be productive and to continue helping people was important to her, regardless of the income from it. "Even though I was making $30 an hour and he could make $30 million in a day," she says, "I thought it was the same impact."

Not that everyone without any need for earned income feels the same way. Middy was called to work with a client once, and when they came face-to-face, they recognized each other as fellow billionairesses. Middy went straight to work, but her peer was uncomfortable.

What are you doing here? the other billionairess asked, almost testily. *You don't need to work, why are you working?!*

Middy explained that she loved her work, so why give it up? In response, she got a lecture from the client, who was increasingly distraught.

I'll still do some work now and then, the billionairess client said, *but never for money!*

Middy was steadfast. She would do things her own way.

At the end of their session together, the client was still discon-
certed over doing business with Middy.

Normally I would tip you, of course, she said. *But I know who
you are . . .*

Middy herself wasn't troubled by the situation.

That's okay, she said. *You can go ahead and give me a tip.*

She didn't get one.

Despite the emphasis Americans put on work, our culture has a
well-established fantasy of not having to work. The first thing that
comes to mind when somebody hits the lottery, maybe after *shopping spree*, is *I don't have to work anymore.*

Yet a lot of lottery winners not only still work, but work at the
same job they had before. A friend of mine had to call road service
one night and got to talking with the serviceman who came out. He
and his wife, a schoolteacher, had won the lottery. They quit their
jobs, hung out for a while . . . and then decided they wanted their
old lives back. She went back to teaching school, he went back to
road service. There are lots of stories like that among lottery winners. Sudden wealth is just not what we think it's going to be.

What those people have discovered is that, despite what most of
us might think, we don't work primarily for money. Yes, we usually
do need the income (and feel like we need a little more than we're
getting), but we probably need an occupation itself more than the
paycheck. Raising children, for instance, although unpaid, is considered a legitimate occupation; but someone else who stays at home
and inexplicably never works tends to raise suspicions. In some
other cultures it is considered rude to ask a stranger "What do you
do?" and it's not standard to have one's job be in the leading line in
obituaries. Americans are conditioned—maybe from the Puritan

work ethic and the fact that the country was built on individual enterprise rather than inherited fortunes—to value hard work, and then to reward ourselves for being productive. We don't enjoy the playtime unless we feel we've first earned it. That causes specific problems for those who have inherited or otherwise come into enough money not to have to work.

The first problem is identification. The question "What do you do?" is dreaded by people who don't have to *do* much of anything, not for money. A magazine for inheritors devoted an issue to work—or not working—and included a list of ways inheritors could answer the inevitable question:

Lie: (In the heat of summer) "I'm a ski instructor." (In January) "I'm a roofer."

Fudge: "I got some money from my family, and I'm taking time off to write children's books." (They don't need to know it's $2 million or that your "time off" has been five years and you've never been published.)

Tell a partial truth: "I coordinate volunteers at the shelter." So what if it's unpaid and only five hours a week?

The independently wealthy can feel the same embarrassment and social dismay that the unintentionally unemployed do when having to reveal that they are not working. On the one hand we fantasize about not having to work, but when it comes down to it, work is prized.

Some of us can get a taste of how some inheritors feel by noticing what happens when we are on vacation or during other downtimes. We think it'll be so great to laze around, and it is for a few days or weeks. Then we often get itchy. We need to *do* something, other than relax or indulge in hobbies. We have a natural urge to be productive, and to function as part of the great societal machine. Retirees often have this same problem: After years of making an important contribution, when they stop working they feel useless.

Since moving here from the Mediterranean, my husband has often lamented, "People here don't know how to relax." When Americans stop for too long, we fear the onset of sloth. How we triumph over it is by working and achieving. And we most often measure our success and achievement by how much money we have earned from our efforts.

Inheritors have a lot of money, so, by American logic, they must have achieved a lot, right? There's the problem. They haven't done diddly for their money, and they know it. They've gotten the reward without having done the work. And yet there is pressure to go about building a career like everyone else. Not to take advantage of the "land of opportunity" in America starts to feel shameful. Here it's about working your way up, and if you're no longer doing that—even if it's because you're a product of one or more generations who *did* work their way up and amassed a fortune doing it—your status is slipping.

Yet when you don't have an economic incentive to develop a career, another hurdle arises: lack of motivation. Most of us prepare for and pursue a life of work because we know we need to support ourselves. When you start out with enough money to live on comfortably, where does the drive come from to work hard at a job? Not that being an inheritor means one is lazy, but lack of motivation and persistence in developing a meaningful and productive career—something most of us take pride in—is a common problem for those who don't need the money. In her book, Thayer Willis describes an inheritor in his late thirties who hadn't been able to launch a career, even though he said he really wanted one: "He realized with a heavy heart that he could only admire—yes, he went through a period of envy—the motivation for earning money that drives most people and which they take entirely for granted. Great careers, he came to understand, have been built on the foundation of necessary income."

As anthropologist Margaret Mead said, "Those American families which settle back to maintain a position of having reached the top in most cases molder there for lack of occupation, ladder-climbers gone stale from sitting too long on the top step."

At the same time, those inheritors who are industrious and set out to build a career can find themselves paralyzed by an overwhelming array of options. In *Born Rich*, Jamie Johnson tries to figure out what to do with his life and asks his father, a recreational painter, for advice. The father, himself an inheritor who never pursued a paying career, seems baffled by his son's question and suggests maybe he could become a collector of documents and such. "Certainly nobody my age would consider collecting maps and documents as a realistic career," the young man says in his commentary. Yet, to indulge his father's advice, Johnson finds an antique-map dealer and sits down with him to discuss the business. When Johnson asks the dealer outright for advice—what would *he* do if he didn't have to work?—the man breaks into incredulous laughter. "Then don't work!" he chortles. "Why would anybody work, if you don't have to?!"

Even a social psychology textbook, which goes on to explain the inherent rewards we get from being part of the working world, reinforces the belief that somebody with enough money to afford full-time leisure wouldn't bother working. It states, "Unless they are fortunate enough to be born with or to acquire vast wealth, most people spend a majority of their waking hours performing some type of job." *But those who are fortunate enough to have wealth*, it is saying, *do not have a job.*

As usual, we are being plagued by a "grass is always greener on the other side of the fence" scenario. While the rest of us glorify the luxury of not having to work, those in that position are mystified by the prospect of full-time leisure. Jessie O'Neill described how miserable her inheritance made her: "I didn't have to work. I didn't have to get up in the morning. I didn't have to do anything. For an average person, that sounds great, but it's only great for a couple of days. Then it's terrifying."

What many of us haven't realized is that the "pursuit of happiness," declared as our inalienable right by Thomas Jefferson and so cherished in our national psyche, is not about the happiness but about the pursuit. The happiness *is* the pursuit.

When I asked Middy how she responds to people who envy her position, she told me quickly, "And I envy my friend who can go off to an island on retreat."

I was confused.

"But you can do that too," I told her. "You can do anything you want to."

"No, I can't. Because I have a husband and I want to be with him, and I have a daughter and I want to spend time with her . . ."

And there are her clients and students whom she wants to be available to help, and at one point during our interviews she was wearing herself out taking a friend back and forth to see doctors. Again she is caretaking, trying to be there for everyone else. Moments that she captures for herself are to spend in nature, or in meditation.

Meditation, or "mindfulness," as a Western version of the practice is called, is something Middy fell in love with years ago. Mindfulness trains you to focus on the present moment with all that it brings to you—pleasure, pain, confusion, anger, bliss—and to accept that moment, and a string of those moments, without any struggle, to indulge them completely.

I took a class in this, so I understand one way in which the practice is so useful to Middy, and to the rest of us, regardless of our life circumstances: It is an equalizer. Meditation breaks you down to the level of a breathing body . . . a heartbeat . . . a combination of particles . . . and then just vibrating energy, a part of the crust and ether of the cosmos. In that state, money makes entirely no difference. Status makes no difference. Possibilities, what you can or can't do, anybody waiting on you or not paying any attention to you at all—none of it makes any meaningful difference. You're throbbing or you're not. (And of course we all are.) When you learn to get into that state, when you're regularly reducing yourself to nothing and everything all at once, you feel a whole new perspective on life and how we experience it. And all of the material surroundings and opportunities that money can buy become mere accessories.

"Life is full of tiny detail," Middy says with appreciation. She still gets as conflicted as the rest of us. She has her moods, and she sometimes becomes overwhelmed and even bottomlessly blue. No amount of wealth can take those conditions away, and sometimes it exacerbates them. But Middy is also at peace. Like when she was floating in the river out west the summer before she met Citizen Q, when the air was heavy and hot and the water was tingly and cold but the combination was somehow perfect: Life offers the pleasantries and the pains in different packages but somehow proportions them equally to each of us.

Middy has been through heart-deflating experiences—some things I haven't told you about—and still she is buoyant, accepting, whole. And not at all because of living in gorgeous properties or having lunch with famous people or driving one of the world's most expensive cars.

"Don't you feel that God has these little feet everywhere?" Middy asked me. "Even the meanest thing, or the most manipulative thing," she said. "It's all out there to give you support. Everyone is there to help you as you need."

CHAPTER SEVEN

⤳

Conclusion

I wish I had known then what I know now. We could have avoided so much angst.

The preoccupation we have with money, and the security and comfort it represents to us, is pretty deeply ingrained, and still baffling. We don't have to pretend that money doesn't matter. It does, to a degree. It can, of course, provide some comfort, some opportunities, some entertainment, some mental and physical respite. We shouldn't be shunning it by any means, nor giving up our striving for more material success, as long as we take pleasure being on that path.

What we need to do is tame money. We need to tame our preoccupation with what other people seem to have, and consciously to dull our fixation on how much better our lives would be if we had more. That is not easily accomplished, however, and I say that from my own experience. How easy it is to slip into feeling some vexation at what someone else has, a touch of greed for what we want for ourselves, and—the worst—the preoccupying belief that getting it will make us, finally, content. It won't.

You can tap into a way of thinking and managing your life that will change your mindset and put you in control of your well-being, no matter what is going on with your finances. Wisdom is out there that is enormously valuable—and right there for the plucking. When I learned about these tools, and started using them in my own life, I became less anxious, more comfortable, happier—all without my financial situation changing. Here's a taste of some of the strategies we can all use to feel better.

What Happened to Us

My recovery started rather strangely, with a book about how to run a marathon. My husband and I are not runners, but at some point in our funk period, my husband brought home a book called *The Non-Runner's Marathon Trainer*. He read the introduction and told me how the authors have taught a marathon class at the University of Northern Iowa, and they promise that anyone—whether they've ever jogged before or not—can complete a marathon by using their four-month training program. It was intriguing, but it sounded farfetched.

Written by a psychology professor and an exercise physiology professor, the book describes a study that they conducted on their students showing how the runners' moods improved over the course of the training and how they became "less tense, angry, depressed, confused and tired and more vigorous and energetic." In conclusion, "Such training seems to increase people's feelings of being in control of their own lives and, from a psychological point of view, we know that feeling that one can influence the events in one's life is part of being psychologically 'hardy' and being able to handle life's stresses and challenges."

I hadn't yet figured out that techniques from sports psychology could be applied to personal finance, but I knew that I had to do *something* that would put me in control of my own well-being. I started the training.

What's powerful about this program is that it trains the mind even more than the body. The average person, the authors explain, even with training, simply cannot access in their bodies the amount of fuel needed to go through the 26.2 miles of a marathon. Then they tell you, however, that you *will* get through it, not because of your body, but because of your mind. Your body can't do it, but your mind can. With the right mental tools and by shaping your mindset through practice, the body will do what the brain says it can. Pretty wild. And, I found out, *very* useful in everyday life.

Sports Psychology

Some of the ways runners and other athletes use psychological training can easily be used in life in general, specifically to conquer, on our own, anxiety over our financial situation.

An incredibly useful sports psychology technique taught through this marathon program is that we need to "create our own reality." That's the key to controlling our environment through our mindset. The idea is to take charge, to develop an "internal locus of control." It means deciding that things are not just happening to you without your having any say in them—you're making them happen.

Sometimes what you're controlling is your reaction to the situation. The marathon folks teach the technique of using the phrase "but it doesn't matter" after every negative thought or disappointment. As the authors suggest, I tried out this technique in other parts of life, at first for little things like when the line at the grocery store was taking forever (*But it doesn't matter!*), and then for more seemingly significant things, like the neighbors jetting to Tahoe for the weekend (*But it definitely doesn't matter!*). In this way, you start training and shaping your mindset so that you can start making life what you want it to be. You can concentrate more on action rather than wasting mental energy on constant reaction, such as the needless anxiety and sulking that come from concerning yourself with the Joneses.

Taking it one step further, the program teaches us to start acting "as if." In marathon terms, that means if you *want* to finish a marathon, start off by believing that you are already a marathoner. That's the reality because you decide on it. The actual reality comes later, and it comes a lot more easily and naturally because you've accepted it as true a long time before. You do that by actually seeing the future reality, in detail, using your mind's eye. This is what athletes are doing when they run through their routines mentally before the actual event.

This kind of mental shaping is worth trying out in your financial life. Start with what you have control over right now, and that's your thoughts, your psychological well-being. As Abraham Lincoln pointed out, "Most folks are about as happy as they make their minds up to be."

As I went through the marathon training program, blindly following all of the sports psychology lessons, my whole life started to change, because I was learning to change my perspective. I realized how the mind could be put to work on our personal finances. Yes, the budget stress was real—but how real? It wasn't that we didn't have a home or couldn't afford groceries or were facing debtor's prison. It's not that our friends and family had shunned us. We were bringing our misery on ourselves, by comparing our situation to a select few people around us; by comparing where we were to where we thought we should be and where we knew we were capable of being; by isolating ourselves and not admitting to others what we were going through; and by imagining others didn't share our stress. We had been creating our own reality, all right, but it was the wrong reality.

Brain Training

The wonderful thing about taking charge of your well-being is that when you do, help comes out of nowhere.

Money matters were still stressing out my husband and me

while he was in school and we were living on one income and taking on tens of thousands of dollars in loans. But once I decided to break out of the holding pattern of just waiting for our life to be "normal" (as if there's any such thing!), things started to come together rather miraculously. It had nothing to do with our finances improving.

I read an article in the *New York Times Magazine* about how Western doctors are studying the physical effects of Buddhist monks' meditating. Intrigued, I searched the Internet for Jon Kabat-Zinn, one of the doctors leading the research. I found out that he has developed a 12-week training program to introduce laypeople to the practice of "mindfulness meditation." One of these courses was being taught at a college within a mile of my home, starting in a few weeks. I signed up.

In the following weeks, the class learned various meditation exercises, different ways of using and being conscious of our minds, and how to make ourselves slow down and take notice of the little things in life. As Thoreau put it in *Walden*, "Why should we live with such hurry and waste of life? We are determined to be starved before we are hungry." Instead, we can change our environment by changing how we're looking at it and responding to it. But it takes practice.

Our meditation teacher talked about using a stress-reduction strategy of confronting problems only when they actually need to be dealt with, rather than wrestling with them repeatedly through imagined scenarios and inside-the-skull sparring. It started to make sense: The mind developed by the marathon program is so powerful when we train it to our advantage, but it can also, off its leash, go to battle against us. That's how we frustrate ourselves when it comes to our finances. We preoccupy ourselves with other people's situations even though they should be irrelevant to us. We construct imaginary worlds of bliss and then pine to belong to them (or sometimes go into debt trying to belong to them). We convince ourselves that contentment is just around the corner, where some other people seem to be already, *and we could join them if we could just get a little further along ourselves.*

What we need is to get a conscious grip on ourselves. And that takes some doing, because real-world forces are working against us.

The Wizard behind the Curtain

We are constantly being manipulated. I won't go into this deeply because this is not news to us; it's just that we could use constant reminders to stay aware of the ways we are being influenced. When we're looking with awareness, we see through it.

To start with, there's marketing. Inspiring us to keep up with the Joneses is an oldie but a goodie in the advertising industry. Actually, they take it a step further: Don't just keep up with others, try to one-up them (*and here's how!*). A recent print ad for a car stated simply, "Ditch the Joneses." This advertising genre extends back at least to the 1910s. The granddaddy was a 1915 Cadillac ad, which ran in the *Saturday Evening Post* and is still hailed today as a piece of advertising genius. It was a block of text titled "The Penalty of Leadership." The car wasn't pictured or even mentioned. Only the Cadillac logo appeared above the text. The essay spoke about how the downside of accomplishing great things is that people will envy you. Here's part of it:

> When a man's work becomes a standard for the whole world, it also becomes a target for the shafts of the envious few. If his work be merely mediocre, he will be left severely alone—if he achieves a masterpiece, it will set a million tongues a-wagging. Jealousy does not protrude its forked tongue at the artist who produces a commonplace painting . . . There is nothing new in this. It is as old as the world and as old as the human passions—envy, fear, greed, ambition, and the desire to surpass. And it all avails nothing.

The ad copy bemoans "the little world" and "spiteful little voices." It *appears* to be ridiculing envy. But what it really inspires is wanting to be one of those leaders, wanting to leave the little people in your wake and have their envy unleashed—at you. Advertising professor James Twitchell explains this legendary ad like this: "If you buy this, you'll change, you'll be special. People will look at you differently. You'll be despised." It appeals to our inner goblin. We'd certainly rather provoke envy in others than suffer from it ourselves.

When we're not worrying about and trying to control how other people will think about us, advertisers play on our concern about our own self-image. *Where should we be in life? How do we know we're successful?* They encourage us to find the answer in buying certain things. A Rolex watch, for example. A radio commercial for Rolex was extremely successful by linking the product to our sense of accomplishment. After a vivid description of you standing on the peak of Mount Everest, the announcer says, "In every life, there is a Mount Everest to be conquered. When you have conquered yours, you'll find your Rolex watch waiting patiently for you to come and pick it up." We are constantly being conditioned to associate achieving success with attaining material goods. Even though I came across this ad in a book about advertising that dissected why it worked so well—and therefore it shouldn't have been able to cast its spell on me—I still find myself, years later, wondering sometimes, *When do I get my Rolex?*

Need I mention credit card offers? How *special* the companies want us to feel for being so responsible that they will give us the privilege of charging on their "exclusive" cards? A pitch I got recently from a card company opened with the line "There's something we don't share with everyone," and closed with the same idea: "This is a feature we offer only to our most highly regarded Cardmembers." *Yeeeah, like those who are not bankrupt?* Oh wait a second, the newly bankrupt are being pitched the same way. A few months after declaring Chapter 13, Dan and Tammy in Florida received a credit card offer that told them, "We think you deserve more credit."

Then there's television and the movies. Are those real lives the people on screen are living? Do the characters live in houses with realistic mortgages and have wardrobes that are appropriate to their occupation and inferred income level? Often not. While it's justifiable because that is part of the entertainment—a make-believe world that looks shinier and more carefree than the reality we ourselves must contend with on a daily basis—it also contributes to building up our dream world, the one we find ourselves trying to live up to even though it doesn't exist.

As for what the media concentrates on, individuals' success stories are featured more often than failures. Americans are optimists. The American Dream is about the upward journey, and we want to be inspired. When we trip or feel we're not measuring up, we withdraw into solitude and silence. So travails and hardship are not detailed nearly as often as accomplishments, especially when it comes to the psychological pressures and social impact of not keeping up, of not getting ahead. It's just not really talked about. Therefore when trouble does come, it can seem like we have been left behind, while all the others have surged ahead. Not true. It helps to keep in mind that what we're hearing and seeing about those around us is a selective slice. Even if we can't see the others or meet them, we do all have plenty of company.

Reality Checks

We must struggle to keep a sense of reality. Just like the marathon program's mantra of *But it doesn't matter*, when the sting of envy hits us, in the midst of our comparisons and surmising, we need to remind ourselves: *Things are not as they seem.* Yank yourself back to reality.

There are some other specific ways to give yourself that yank. One is by using relativity to your advantage. Expose yourself to those who are worse off. As a social psychology textbook explains,

"Downward comparisons can increase self-esteem and reduce stress."
When I find myself feeling blue (*still!*) about not being far enough
ahead financially, I put myself in the place of someone living in the
housing projects a few blocks from us. To them, our income is *more
than* more than enough, our apartment is luxurious, our lifestyle
enviable. They, in turn, are fortunate in the eyes of others. They
have their own apartments, they have food in the refrigerator, the
tap water is sanitary, they have free access to the Internet and
to books at the library—more than many others have. Except for
pockets of extreme poverty even in the United States, the standard
of living here, traditionally measured, is far above most of the rest of
the world's population.

Now is a good time to point out something the poor have that
most of us don't. Because the poor are so stretched for resources,
they tend to do less comparing and contrasting and more sharing
and supporting. A book about unemployment points to urban
anthropologists who explain how poor communities have developed "complex networks of exchange partners," including siblings,
cousins, neighbors, and family friends, to share child care, clothing,
food, money, and furniture among themselves as needed. Everyone
needs the help, and it's obvious, so they help one another rather than
compete. Even though they have fewer material resources, they
apparently don't work themselves into a psychological pretzel over
getting ahead of the Joneses. This brings to mind something I found
in the thesaurus under *crisis*. It's a quote describing crisis as "God's
call to us to reach a new level of humanity."

Another way to reach out to reality is by giving. You're well off.
You are. You have more than others do, and you have more than
you need to get by. So contribute some of what you have. Share
your time, talents, and resources with an individual or organization
that needs you. Make yourself useful to society, even if you are just
one droplet on the windowpane. And don't be a martyr about it—
do it your way, so you get personal pleasure out of it too. Don't vol-

unteer at the soup kitchen if that doesn't genuinely appeal to you, and don't write a check to just any charity. Make it something you believe in and are truly motivated to help, something that makes you feel good.

Don't just help others, but help yourself. That's right, indulge yourself. It's not only okay, it's essential to your well-being. Some of us have to fight a tendency toward extravagance and greed, true, but others have to fight behaving like sacrificial lambs. Our culture sometimes praises too highly giving to others while frowning on taking for ourselves. Go ahead and take some for yourself. You know the biblical instruction to "love thy neighbor as thyself"? A rabbi pointed out that while we hear that and put the emphasis on loving others, the equally important part is loving yourself. You can't love your neighbor as you do yourself, he said, if you don't first love yourself.

Our yoga teacher spoke about the importance of taking care of *yourself*. "You have to cheer for yourself," she said, "because sometimes you're going to be the only one. And if you don't do it, who will?" Make some time for yourself, and give to yourself. Deliberately seek out even brief moments of joy—no matter what the external circumstances—and bring beauty and excitement into your life however you can. We each have to customize our buffet. Just follow your version of the instruction that "when all you have left in the world is two loaves of bread, sell one and buy hyacinths for the soul."

Now, I know that sometimes you're in no mood to cheer yourself up, especially if you are burdened by money problems. One thing that might help, even when you're in what you see as dire straits (which is relative, of course), is again to widen your perspective. In his book detailing the Debtors Anonymous program, Jerrold Mundis tells those feeling crushed by debts, "Right now, at this very moment, you have: 1. A roof over your head, 2. Clothes to wear, 3. Food to eat. So right now, today, you are perfectly all right—you have everything you need, you don't lack for anything essential." When you focus on the gloom and doom of the situation, you magnify it. You let your thoughts and imagination beat you down, even though you don't have to. Instead, you can use your mindset to make yourself feel better, to improve your situation just by how you look at it. As the self-help folks say, you can't always control or change the situation, but you can control and change how you respond to the situation. Master the part you do have control over, and let the rest of it fall into place. (Granted, when you take that too far, you end up in denial. You have to find the helpful midpoint between ignoring a financial issue you really need to attend to and letting the problem mentally mushroom.)

You have to search for new ways of looking at your situation. When it comes to the Joneses, another weapon you can use against envy is, selectively, to embrace it. Yes, it's a sin and it's supposed to feel awful when it strikes. But there is, as always, another way to look at it, another way to conquer it rather than trying to smother it. It goes like this: When you envy, you want something someone else has. You are filled by desire. Desire is actually one of the finer things in life. You need it to experience passion. It can inspire you to move toward what you want, it can energize you, it can lead to progress. Desire is the fuel for the pursuit of happiness. You try to get what you want, that's how you have fun. A grandson of Cornelius Vanderbilt complained of his inherited fortune, "It has left me with nothing to hope for, with nothing definite to seek or strive for." Fortunately most of us don't have that problem. What we are blessed with is the full thrill of the hunt, the thrill of the pursuit.

Thankfulness

In the midst of our pursuit, however, another reality check comes in super handy: gratitude. This is really an all-purpose fixer. It has been argued that cultivating gratitude is the only way truly to adjust your happiness barometer. It's a version of looking on the bright side, but it calls specifically for feeling thankful. This is something we should all be doing on at least a daily basis: enumerating some of the things that are going right. Many of us hear early on in life to "count our blessings," but maybe we forget. Even when things truly do seem to suck from all sides, for that is when we are very tempted to dismiss exercises like this, you can start by coming up with one thing to be grateful for. Or maybe . . . two? Get the gratitude rolling, and you'll find a better mood brewing. The more you do it, the more you'll notice your perspective shifting toward the positive. The Joneses, and whatever image we are struggling to live up to, start to fade when we recognize on a consistent basis how far we've come and what we already have, right now. To have some fun with it, take a tiptoe over to the Joneses' side of the fence and try to look at your life as others see it: What do you have, what *are* you, that they could (and maybe do) envy? Be grateful for that. Envy your own life for a change.

Abundance

Not to keep coming back to the doldrums, but I keep thinking about the worst-case scenario, about the times we feel not just the self-induced tug of inferiority but the heat of fiscal meltdown. After all, what works under those circumstances has to be good for pretty much all occasions, right? So here's something else I learned during the tough times my husband and I experienced, and from the wisdom that started coming into our lives as soon as we opened our minds to it: The universe will provide. You'll get what you really need as you need it.

That might sound a little farfetched, but it's real. There's not a logical explanation as to how it works, but when you have faith in the concept it does work. In his book *Creating Affluence*, Deepak Chopra tells how, when planning a world peace project, somebody asked this yogi, "Where is all the money going to come from?" And the yogi replied, "From wherever it is at the moment."

When you think about your own life, you can probably find examples of how this has already happened. Just what you needed shows up, inexplicably. Specifically, when you need it, and are open to it, money flows to you. I was explaining this belief to my sister one day at lunch, and since she is very straightforward and practical, I expected her to give me a raised eyebrow. Instead she said, "That's so true!" She described how when our other sister moved across the country, she wondered how she would afford to buy plane tickets to visit her all the time. Just then, she was offered a part-time job for a few hours per week, which gave her just the extra money she needed for the travel. (This lasted for two years, until our sister moved back. Mysteriously, the part-time job dried up a month later.)

A friend who makes less money than most people do was telling me that she gives 10 percent of her gross income to the church. She said that she could not afford to do it, especially when she had first decided to tithe. At that time she was making, as she described it, "pennies." She had a student loan payment to make every month, she helped out her younger sister, at lunch she couldn't pay for a sandwich from the deli. But she was determined to give to the church before anything else was paid, and so she did. What happened after that is something a lot of other people have described too: The money or thing she needed just showed up, every time. A check she wasn't expecting came in the mail, a friend gave her something she was going to have to buy, work went into overtime so she earned extra income. Somehow, each month, everything always worked out. The universe provided.

Part of the universe providing, however, requires that we recognize and accept the help when it comes. Middy enjoyed telling me a story she had heard from the Native Americans: A village is flooding and a man is in his house. Another villager comes by and says to the man in the house, *You can't stay here! Come with me!*

No, the man says. *God will save us.*

The villager walks on. The water rises past the first floor, and the man climbs to the second floor of his house. Other villagers come by the man's window in a boat.

Come on, they say, *this is the end! Come with us!*

No, I believe in God, and he will help me, the man insists.

The villagers must paddle on. The water rises, and now the man is on his roof. A helicopter arrives and hovers above.

Come on, you have to come with us! You'll drown!

No, God will save me.

But the water rises past the man's roof and he drowns. Then he complains to God, *God, I trusted you and you let me down!*

Give me a break! God responds. *I sent you a man, I sent you a boat, I sent you a helicopter!*

Sometimes the seed of just what you need is planted in the misfortune itself. During trying times, about the last thing you feel up to is wondering what good is coming of it. But developing some faith in this concept will help you get through crises and funks.

After I met Dan and Tammy and had been interviewing them about their bankruptcy, one evening a friend and I went out to a Japanese tea ceremony demonstration and talk. I had known about this class for years and had always wanted to go but had never made the reservation. Despite feeling like I didn't have any time to spare, suddenly I signed up and we went.

Then, as the world works, in the middle of the tea class it hit me why I was meant to be there. When I got home I was excited to call Dan and Tammy and tell them what had happened in the tea temple. I felt like it might, in some way, help them put their bankruptcy in perspective.

What happened is this: The elderly Japanese man who teaches the tea ceremony class explained to us that tea bowls in Japan are very expensive, routinely $1,000. The best ones are considered art. Once a tea bowl sold at an auction for $1 million, our teacher said, and more impressive was that the man who bought it wasn't just looking at it but was using it to drink tea! "Can you imagine," the teacher said gently as he cupped his hands and rocked the imaginary tea bowl in front of him, "a million dollars moving back and forth, back and forth?" Then he started to giggle. "Can you imagine the moment the bowl dropped and broke?" He paused. We felt the pain of the million-dollar bowl shattering. Then the teacher said through his smile, "Can you imagine the *freedom* of that moment?"

Making the First Move

So those are some things we can work at on our own to take charge of our well-being, no matter how much money we have or owe or want. We can also work toward cracking the money taboo. We can ease out of the closet, be more honest, ask more questions, share our concerns.

This is, as you know, easier said than done. But it's well worth working toward, bit by bit, because this secrecy and mystery, these fibs and fronts about our money, are making us all worse off.

Couples counselors talk about the importance of *someone* making the first move. I think it's the same with talk about money. Take a step toward being honest: Next time you're about to let a half-truth slip out, just don't. Tell it how it really is. Or admit how uncomfortable it is to talk about it, and ask if the other person feels the same. (They do.) Then step back and see how people respond. When I told people I was writing about keeping up with the Joneses, some of them scrambled right out of the rabbit hole. With the subject in the open, they admitted that they couldn't figure out how their best friends could afford their lifestyle, how they felt inferior to their siblings who made more money, how in one case my friend lied to his parents about his job because he was ashamed of not earning more and needing to moonlight. Even the really *nice* people, the ones you'd swear wish for the Joneses' good fortune even before their own, given the opportunity, they too sniped. *Oh my*, the things that tumble out when people consider it safe to talk! We need to hear it, because we need to understand how alike we all are, and to see how things are never as they seem.

So we can curb our own propaganda that we put out into the world, and we can nudge others in the same direction. However, some people, as you can guess, will not be nudged. The taboo is strong, and we are so used to defining ourselves by our financial status that we are afraid to expose any weaknesses related to money. Still, try never to be discouraged by . . . how to put it . . . *the jerk factor*. That will always be there. An editor of mine said it best when I complained about an uncooperative source: "The world is full of jerks, ranging from the merely annoying to the bloodthirsty." Braggers, those who savor the thought of igniting our envy, the ones who would rush to buy a Cadillac after reading that ad, fall roughly into this category. Just ignore them. You're too busy for their nonsense.

Getting Out There

There are some places you can go where money is being discussed. One of them is Debtors Anonymous, which isn't only for people in debt but for anyone who feels out of control over his or her financial life and wants to be more at peace with it. I was amazed how many meetings this organization has. In Manhattan there are around ten meetings a day, seven days a week, as early as seven in the morning and as late as eight at night. *Who are all these people?* I had to wonder. Like those in Alcoholics Anonymous, there is no typical profile. The best way to describe whom you're likely to come face-to-face with in a DA meeting is: someone like yourself. We keep our money issues so hidden, you can't tell who is troubled. It's the same story credit counselors and bankruptcy attorneys tell, that they have successful doctors and high-earning business owners coming in for help alongside those with more modest incomes.

I would like to have gotten inside DA and talked with some members, but when I got in touch with them in New York and asked if I could come to a meeting or at least talk with someone involved, the response was an identity-masked e-mail telling me to stay away. Whoever it was behind the mask—whom I reached via their e-mail address for press inquiries!—wrote to me that they take the anonymous part very seriously. It is certainly testament to the strength of the money taboo in our society that an organization designed to help people deal openly with money issues wouldn't put forward a single person willing to speak about it. Granted, the second time they turned me down, they noted, "Remember, we're here for you if you or anyone you know ever really needs us." So I'll pass that much along. Any group in which people are encouraged to speak frankly about their financial lives makes progress toward facing up to the taboo. In lieu of personal observation, I can recommend Jerrold Mundis's inspiring book, *How to Get Out of Debt, Stay Out of Debt & Live Prosperously*, which is based on his own experiences with DA.

It might not be any easier for you to show up at one of those meetings, though, than it was for me to get in the door. The social stigma we imagine attached to a group for debtors is enough to keep many people far away, no matter how much they need it. When I suggested to Dan in Florida that he and Tammy might check out DA, he quickly dismissed the idea: "I really can't see myself standing up at a meeting and saying, 'I'm Dan and I'm a debtor.'" First, that's not how you introduce yourself at DA, and second, so what? The last place you would expect to be judged and criticized, as Tammy feared their friends might do, is at a meeting where other intrepid souls have come for support. This is a sort of reverse keeping up with the Joneses phenomenon at work: Instead of thinking others have it better than we do, we insist we can't possibly be as bad off as *them*. We need to get over those comparisons on both sides. If money problems are making you miserable, it very well might help to meet others and talk, or at least hear their experiences.

If overabundance is your issue—and it is for some—there's a group for that too. More than Money, based in Massachusetts, organizes discussion groups in certain cities where members can talk about the concerns of having plenty of money. Past topics, inspired by their quarterly magazine, include How much to give? Does money make people happy? and Who knows you're rich?

Another place money talk is going on, to a degree, is at Financial Peace University, a three-month class and discussion group held regularly around the country. The program is Christian-based (meaning there is an occasional quotation from the Bible), so the meetings are often held in churches, but it is open and relevant to people of any faith. The class was developed by Dave Ramsey, someone who went from having no money to being a millionaire to going bankrupt to becoming a (multi)millionaire again. The format of the class is to learn in a larger group about financial topics such as cash flow management, insurance, and investing, then to break into smaller sections for guided discussion.

I attended the course at a church in Queens, and my experience was that in terms of unburdening yourself and finding personal support, the class is as helpful as you make it. When I stood up and told a group of strangers about struggling to get by on one income, I saw a lot of nods, and that alone was a huge relief. Early on, another young woman stood up and declared that she had $40,000 worth of credit card debt, mostly from catalog shopping, but she was determined to tackle it. We clapped to encourage her. An older man admitted to blowing $1,500 that he couldn't afford on gambling in Atlantic City. Who among us hasn't done some version of that, and it was helpful to hear the confession.

At other times, what happened in the class was what happens in life: People jumped up to share success stories more readily than setbacks. That's supposed to be inspirational, and sometimes it was, but not always. One woman stood up and shared the good news that she had put the first step of the program into action three weeks before and had saved $500 in her emergency fund. That weekend her pipes had frozen and the emergency repair bill came to $480. "It worked!" she told us happily. Except it didn't make the woman sitting in front of me very happy. She turned to her friend and whispered exasperatedly, "Five hundred dollars? *In three weeks?!*" She sighed and her shoulders drooped. If you do take one of these courses or something similar, get the most out of it by letting the others know what your issues are, what's making you nervous, and what you're working toward. Others will be in the same boat, and being honest helps both you and them. Be brave and get it out there.

Not that the Financial Peace class is meant as group therapy, but generally speaking, confession is good for us. Numerous studies have shown that writing or talking about stressful or disturbing events in our lives has both psychological and physical benefits. Keeping everything to ourselves, alternatively, can be damaging. "Not disclosing thoughts and feelings over time, then, is correlated with disease and mortality," summarizes one journal article, titled "The Psychophysiology of Confession." The studies that have been done often look at disclosing traumas like abuse, and they correlate higher rates of disease, elevated blood pressure, and other illnesses to not confiding. Money is such a big part of our lives that I would guess that keeping financial stress and trauma secret eats away at us in a similar way.

Another place to turn to commiserate with others is the intimate anonymity of the Internet. It's no coincidence that this is where I turned when I needed support, and it's where Dan turned and it's where Middy turned. We expect the Internet, and the community we know is out there, to solve our problems when nobody nearer to us can. If you want to discuss the personal and social side of finances, rather than the usual investment strategies or tips on saving, meet online at www.greenwithenvythebook.com.

In stepping forward to make changes in how you think about your personal financial situation and how we talk to one another about it, in confronting the taboo, keep in mind something the anthropologist Margaret Mead said: "We *are* our culture." The taboo lives because we are keeping it alive by following it. When we act boldly, when we make our own decisions about what we'll talk about and how we'll view things, we improve our own culture.

About Next Door . . .

You know how I mentioned it's easy to slip back into noticing and caring when we see others around us looking better off financially? The couple next door to us moved out, just when we had come really to know and understand them and be comfortable with them as our next-door partners. The nice thing was, we had another shot at digesting someone new moving in and never wondering about their business.

However. It turned into déjà vu, except with a higher price tag on the apartment. A young couple our age was buying the place. They were paying cash. We heard it was family money. Forget how we heard, but we *heard*. We even heard how much the family fortune was—or, correction, was *said to be*.

We were amazed by how similar the situation was. The wife even got pregnant shortly after moving in. *Am I being tested?* I wondered. You're not going to believe this, but they even got a ton of packages delivered. (*Does* everyone *do so much shopping by mail, or is it only whoever happens to move in next door to us?*)

We ordered in for dinner one night. When my husband went to the door and took the food from the delivery man, he noticed something in the hallway. He turned to me, gave a nod toward the new neighbors' apartment, and asked sort of covertly, *Have you seen this?*

I thought I had, but I joined him at our door to look out anyway. Ah yes, I'd seen it, but it had grown since the afternoon. We stood together peeking around the corner at the neighbors' door, which looked like a Christmas tree for all of the packages stacked up in front of it. (Away on vacation, *and* getting deliveries. *Hmph.*) Then my husband ushered us back inside and closed the door. We started laughing.

It didn't matter.

Endnotes

Chapter One: Green with Envy

Quote from anthropologist Margaret Mead: Margaret Mead, *And Keep Your Powder Dry: An Anthropologist Looks at America* (New York: W. Morrow and Co., 1942).

Quote from psychologist Anita Weinreb Katz: Alex Williams, "To Have and Have More," *New York Magazine* (June 14, 1999).

Flea research cited in class "Launching New Ventures" taught by Clifford Schorer, Columbia Business School, New York.

The American capitalist economy being driven by the creation of desire and discontent outlined in Paul Wachtel's *The Poverty of Affluence: A Psychological Portrait of the American Way of Life* (New York: Free Press, 1983); and in John Kenneth Galbraith's *The Affluent Society* (Boston: Houghton Mifflin, 1958).

Survey on achieving the American Dream: "Harper's Index," *Harper's Magazine* 277, no. 1661 (1988): 15.

Statistic on living paycheck to paycheck: "America Saves," survey by Princeton Survey Research Associates for the Consumer Federation of America (December 20, 2000).

American Psychological Association survey on money: "As Tax Deadline Approaches Americans Say Money Is Number One Cause of Stress," APA press release (March 31, 2004).

Statistic on credit card debt: Federal Reserve Statistical Release G.19, "Consumer Credit," (January 9, 2006).

Survey on debts making home life unhappy: Consolidated Credit Counseling Service 2004 Survey.

Quote from research in *The Overspent American*: Juliet B. Schor, *The Overspent American: Why We Want What We Don't Need* (New York: HarperPerennial, 1999), 215. (Research results are from Schor's own survey.)

Research showing couples in bankruptcy more likely to file for divorce: Elizabeth Warren and Amelia Warren Tyagi, *The Two-Income Trap: Why Middle-Class Mothers and Fathers Are Going Broke* (New York: Basic Books, 2003).

Quote from book by anthropologist on downward mobility: Katherine Newman, *Falling from Grace: The Experience of Downward Mobility in the American Middle Class* (New York: Vintage Books, 1989).

Harvard and University of Miami survey about income: Sara J. Solnick and David Hemenway, "Is More Always Better?: A Survey of Positional Concerns," *Journal of Economic Behavior and Organization* 37, no. 3 (1998): 373–383.

British experiment on relative wealth using computer gambling game: Daniel John Zizzo and Andrew Oswald, "Are People Willing to Pay to Reduce Others' Incomes?" The Warwick Economics Research Paper Series, Department of Economics, University of Warwick (July 2, 2001).

Princeton experiment with two players and accepting payoffs: Alan G. Sanfey, James K. Rilling, Jessica A. Aronson, et al., "The Neural Basis of Economic Decision-Making in the Ultimatum Game," *Science* 300, no. 5626 (2003): 1755–1758.

Survey of Americans earning more than $100,000 per year: Schor, *Overspent American*, 6.

Chapter Two: The Money Next Door

Money magazine survey results reported in Scott Medintz, "Secrets, Lies and Money," *Money* (April 2005): 121–128.

Quote from *Salon*: Scott Rosenberg, "Introducing Salon Money Week," *Salon.com* (October 27, 1997).

Quote from New York City sermon on money as taboo: Stephen P. Bauman, "The Last Taboo," Christ Church (October 12, 2003).

Quote from psychologist on money as taboo: Richard Trachtman, "The Money Taboo: Its Effects in Everyday Life and in the Practice of Psychotherapy," *Clinical Social Work Journal* 27, no. 3 (1999): 275–288.

Quotes from Jamie Johnson about code of silence among the wealthy and about being a traitor: from Julia Chaplin, "Biting the Silver Spoon That Feeds Him, on Film," *New York Times* (October 12, 2003).

Explanations of etiquette from Peggy Post, *Emily Post's Etiquette*, 16th edition (New York: HarperCollins, 1997).

Quote on discussion of money in the Bible from the Reverend Bauman's sermon "The Last Taboo," cited above. Other quote, on congregants not discussing their finances, from personal interview.

Quote from sermon on why we don't discuss money: Mark D. Morrison-Reed, "The Taboo," First Unitarian Congregation of Toronto (October 21, 2001).

Freud's discussion of money's legacy of being dirty: Sigmund Freud, "Character and Anal Erotism," *The Freud Reader* (New York: W.W. Norton & Company, 1989), 296–297.

Quote from Emma Jung's letter to Freud: Sigmund Freud and C.G. Jung, *The Freud/Jung Letters* (Princeton University Press, 1994), 203.

Psychologist Richard Trachtman's quote about Freud: Trachtman, "The Money Taboo," cited above.

Quote from Manhattan therapist: personal interview.

New York Times Magazine article on Debtors Anonymous experience: Carol Lloyd, "Cents and Sensibility," *New York Times Magazine* (December 28, 1997): 50.

List of problems that money has been identified as a potential root of: from Trachtman, "The Money Taboo," cited above. Also his quote about money being an ignored subject.

Quotes from psychologist David Lansky from his article "Money and Meaning: 'Psychologically Informed' Planning," *Journal of Practical Estate Planning* (February/March 2003).

Quote from Howard Dvorkin about spouses hiding credit card debt: personal interview.

Chapter Three: Keeping Up with the Joneses

In reconstructing Dan and Tammy's financial downfall, I used bankruptcy court documents in addition to personal interviews.

Comparisons to national and neighborhood medians and educational attainment: Census Bureau data of the relevant years.

Comparison to national median incomes by education level: Department of Education data of the relevant year.

Quotes from Federal Reserve and statistics on home equity lending and borrowing: Glenn Canner, Thomas Durkin, and Charles Luckett, "Recent Developments in Home Equity Lending," *Federal Reserve Bulletin* (April 1998).

More Americans buying homes but owning less of them: Javier Silva, "A House of Cards: Refinancing the American Dream," briefing paper published by Demos: A Network for Ideas & Action (January 9, 2005).

Statistics on savings and credit card debt as percentages of income: "The New Bankruptcy Epidemic: Forecasts, Causes and Risk Control," SMR Research Corp. (2001): 14, 94. Calculated with income figures from U.S. Department of Commerce and debt figures from the Federal Reserve.

Statistics on 1990s growth of credit card debt: Tamara Draut and Javier Silva, "Borrowing to Make Ends Meet: The Growth of Credit Card Debt in the '90s," briefing paper published by Demos: A Network for Ideas & Action (September 8, 2003).

Statistic on average number of Visas and MasterCards per household: *The Nilson Report*, issue 828 (February 2005); I divided the 566 million cards in circulation reported in Nilson by 106 million U.S. households.

The difference between self-reported credit card debt and industry-reported statistic: Draut and Silva, "Borrowing to Make Ends Meet." Calculations based on comparing data from Federal Reserve's 2001 Survey of Consumer Finances with the Federal Reserve data on outstanding revolving credit (i.e., credit cards).

Quote from Federal Reserve report: Thomas Durkin, "Credit Cards: Use and Consumer Attitudes, 1970–2000," *Federal Reserve Bulletin* (September 2000).

Discussion of credit card lending practices and terms: Draut and Silva, "Borrowing to Make Ends Meet."

Impression management and self-deception: Robert A. Baron and Donn Erwin Byrne, *Social Psychology: Understanding Human Interaction* (Boston: Allyn and Bacon, 1991).

Quotes from bankruptcy attorney Glenn: personal interview.

Information on Chapter 7 and Chapter 13 bankruptcy: Nolo (www.nolo.com), American Bankruptcy Institute (www.abiworld.org), and attorney Glenn.

Information from Consumer Bankruptcy Project: Elizabeth Warren, Jay Lawrence Westbrook, and Teresa A. Sullivan, *The Fragile Middle Class: Americans in Debt* (New Haven, CT: Yale University Press, 2000); and Elizabeth Warren and Amelia Warren Tyagi, *The Two-Income Trap: Why Middle-Class Mothers and Fathers Are Going Broke* (New York: Basic Books, 2003).

An insignificant percentage of people take advantage of the bankruptcy system: A resident scholar at the American Bankruptcy Institute estimated that fewer than 3 percent of filers could repay their debts but still filed bankruptcy.

Discussion of change in bankruptcy court policies: attorney Glenn; and Department of Justice, Executive Office for United States Trustees, "U.S. Trustee Program Launches Bankruptcy Civil Enforcement Initiative," press release (October 30, 2001).

Discussion of 2005 bankruptcy reform: Nolo (www.nolo.com), American Bankruptcy Institute (www.abiworld.org), and attorney Glenn.

Quote on new bankruptcy law by California law firm's Web site: Moran Law Group (www.moranlaw.net).

Statistics comparing numbers of bankruptcies to divorces and college graduates: U.S. Bankruptcy Courts (1.6 million personal bankruptcies in 2003 and 2004); Centers for Disease Control, National Vital Statistics Reports (1.1 million divorces in 2003 and 2004); Department of Education, National Center for Educational Statistics (1.3 million bachelor degrees earned in 2003).

Researcher who studied bankrupt families: Deborah K. Thorne, *Personal Bankruptcy through the Eyes of the Stigmatized: Insight into Issues of Shame, Gender and Marital Discord* (doctoral dissertation, Washington State University, 2001).

Book based on the findings of the Consumer Bankruptcy Project: Warren and Tyagi, *The Two-Income Trap*. The quotes that follow are taken from this book, pps. 212, 177.

Quotes from Deborah Thorne are from her dissertation, cited above.

Quote from social psychology textbook and discussion of cognitive dissonance: Baron and Byrne, *Social Psychology*.

Chapter Four: Capitol Secrets

All quotes from unnamed sources are from personal interviews with former members of Congress.

Quotes and information from Jack Buechner: personal interview.

Quinn's story and quotes: personal interviews with Jack Quinn and Jack Quinn III.

Newspaper article headline "Congress's Millionaires—A Thriving Breed": Jeffery L. Sheler with Robert Barr, *U.S. News and World Report* (June 3, 1985).

Newspaper article headline "Lawmakers Don't Feel Your Pain": Shannon Buggs, *Houston Chronicle* (May 16, 2005).

Quotes from Al Gore's campaign consultant (Bill Knapp) and Bob Kerrey: Sally Quinn, "It's Full of Corruption, Partisanship and Elitism. At Least, It's That Way Until People Move Here," *Washington Post* (April 12, 2001).

Quotes from Sam Gejdenson: personal interview.

Anecdote and quote from Tom Foley: Quinn, "Full of Corruption."

Myths about congressional retirement benefits: see urban legend debunking site www.snopes.com.

Quote from *Tampa Tribune* article about platinum parachutes: Keith Epstein, "When Career's Over, Politicians Spared Retirees' Usual Worries," *Tampa Tribune* (December 19, 2004).

Quote from Steve Tomaszewski: personal interview.

Congressional salary figure is as of 2005.

Net worths of Edward Kennedy, Jay Rockefeller, and Jon Corzine: Matthew Murray, "The 50 Richest Members of Congress," *Roll Call* (September 12, 2005).

Quote from *Houston Chronicle* on members being millionaires: Buggs, "Lawmakers Don't Feel Your Pain."

For more about the pay, benefits, and regulations of congressional compensation, see the Congressional Institute's Web site, www.conginst.org.

Characterizations of members' finances taken from review of publicly available financial disclosure documents, available from the Center for Responsive Politics, www.opensecrets.org.

Quote from New York newspaper article about credit card debt: Paul Vitello, "Bankruptcy Bill Could Be Debt of Us," *Newsday* (March 13, 2005).

Recent accounts of the Animal House owned by George Miller: Johanna
 Neuman, "At This 'Animal House,' the Party Is Democratic," *Los
 Angeles Times* (July 25, 2005); Katherine Marsh, "Chuck's Place,"
 New York Times (March 3, 2002).
Quote from Dick Durbin about the size of the rats: Marsh, "Chuck's Place."
Quote from Al Franken: Andrea Estes, "Delahunt, Roommates Are Sit-
 com Fodder," *Boston Globe* (December 2, 2001).
Anecdote about Marty Russo billing for new tires: Marsh, "Chuck's Place."
Information about members sleeping in their offices: personal interviews
 with members or their press secretaries.
Cost of congressional races: Center for Responsive Politics.
For further discussion on the logistics and costs of members' families relo-
 cating to Washington, D.C., see Lou Frey Jr. and Michael T. Hayes,
 editors, *Inside the House: Former Members Reveal How Congress
 Really Works* (Lanham, MD: U.S. Association of Former Members of
 Congress and United Press of America, 2001).
Statistic on members carrying credit card debt: Josephine Hearn, "A Hill of
 Credit-Card Debt: Some Lawmakers Juggle Cards and Up to $250k
 Owed," *The Hill* (March 10, 2005), data from financial disclosures
 covering 2003.
Quote from Tim Bishop: J. Jioni Palmer, "Local Congressmen Reap Credit
 Card Debt," *Newsday* (March 14, 2005).
Quote on debt of Jan Schakowsky and Melissa Bean: Illinois Republican
 Party, "Reps. Bean, Schakowsky's Personal Spending Habits Should
 Worry Taxpayers," *US Fed News* (March 10, 2005).
Anecdote about a member's suitcase popping open at baggage claim: Frey
 and Hayes, *Inside the House*, 70–71.
Quote from Bill Pascrell: Ed Henry, "Sex in the City," *Roll Call* (Novem-
 ber 8, 2001).

Chapter Five: Baby Boomers Beware
Statistics on rates of college attendance: "The Inheritor," *Time* (January 6,
 1967). This was the cover story naming boomers "Man of the Year."
Quotes from Scott Wetzler: personal interview.
Quote about tyranny from member of Harvard Class of 1977: Bo Emerson,
 "The Burden of Expectations," *Atlanta Journal-Constitution* (July 8,
 2002).

Quotes from Daphne Merkin: Daphne Merkin, *Dreaming of Hitler: Passions & Provocations* (New York: Crown, 1997).

Quotes from class notes: from recent issues of Ivy League alumni magazines.

For more on boomer earnings, wealth, inheritances, and inequality: Michael J. Weiss, "GREAT Expectations: Boomer Wealth Forecasts Wilt," *American Demographics* (May 1, 2003); Mary Elizabeth Hughes and Angela M. O'Rand, "The Lives and Times of the Baby Boomers," report published by the Russell Sage Foundation and the Population Reference Bureau (2004).

Quote from *American Demographics* on boomers not inheriting: Weiss, "GREAT Expectations."

Statistics about boomer spending: Bureau of Labor Statistics, 2003 Consumer Expenditure Survey.

Boomers having highest credit card balances: Federal Reserve, 2001 Survey of Consumer Finances.

Boomer vacations: Sally S. Stich, "Breaking Away: Holidaying Boomers Leave Rituals and Stress Behind," *Time* (September 4, 2005).

Boomers putting in pools and quote from pool industry report: Alan Naditz, "The Big Boom: For Baby Boomers, Buying a Pool or Spa Is a Case of Image," *Pool & Spa News* (November 21, 2001).

Boomers more likely to be taking on debt than paying it down, and quote from think tank about boomer expenditures: Tamara Draut and Heather C. McGhee, "Retiring in the Red," briefing paper published by Demos: A Network for Ideas & Action (February 2004).

Information on boomerangers and permaparenting: Kim Campbell, "More Graduates Opt to Live with Mom and Dad," *Christian Science Monitor* (July 9, 2001).

Quote from *Psychology Today* on permaparenting: Pamela Paul, "The Permaparent Trap: By Housing Their Twenty-Something Children and Financing Their Lives, Today's Parents May Be Compromising Their Own," *Psychology Today* (September/October 2003).

Indirect quote from president of a national credit counseling agency: Howard Dvorkin, Consolidated Credit Counseling Services, personal interview.

Work being the pension of the poor: Steve Lohr, "The Late, Great 'Golden Years,'" *New York Times* (March 6, 2005).

Survey about boomers working into retirement age because they need the money: press release from annual Del Webb survey, "Many Baby

Boomers Have New Homes, Money on Their Minds," *Business Wire* (June 7, 2005). This is also the survey showing healthcare a top financial concern.

Statistics on medical care expenditures: National Bureau of Economic Research.

Statistic on a third of large companies offering insurance: Kaiser Family Foundation and the Health Research and Educational Trust, "Employer Health Benefits 2005 Annual Survey."

Statistics on net worth and assets: Federal Reserve, 2001 Survey of Consumer Finances.

Statistics on ownership and balances of retirement accounts: "401(k)-Type Plan and IRA Ownership," Employee Benefit Research Institute (January, 2005). Figures are as of 2002 and derived from the Census Bureau's Survey of Income and Program Participation.

AARP survey of Americans over 45 and quotes: "Perspectives Past, Present and Future: Traditional and Alternative Financial Practices of the 45+ Community," AARP (2005).

Quotes from sociologist Erving Goffman: Erving Goffman, *Interaction Ritual* (Garden City, NY: Anchor Books, 1967).

Quote from psychologist Martin Seligman: Martin Seligman, "Boomer Blues: With Too Great Expectations, the Baby-Boomers Are Sliding into Individualistic Melancholy," *Psychology Today* (October 1988).

Statistic on suicide rates among the youth and elderly: National Center for Injury Prevention and Control at the Centers for Disease Control and Prevention.

Quotes from Bo Emerson: Emerson, "Burden of Expectations."

Median income statistic from Harvard Class of 1977: Jason Weeden, John Sabini, Melanie C. Green, et al., "The Harvard & Radcliffe Class of 1977 Longitudinal Study: 25th Reunion Report," Harvard-Radcliffe Class of 1977.

Information on retiring in Central and South America: Linda Stern, "Money: Running Away to Retire," *Newsweek* (March 14, 2005); Shabnam Mogharabi, "Latin Fever: Baby Boomers Are Retiring South of the Border," *Pool & Spa News* (November 1, 2004).

Chapter Six: Behind the Hedges
Statistic on number of New Yorkers making more than $500,000: Daniel Gross, "Don't Hate Them Because They're Rich," *New York*

Magazine (April 18, 2005). The Census Bureau's American Community Survey 2004 estimates the number of Manhattan residents making more than $200,000 at 78,403.

New York Times article about making $200,000: Alex Williams, "Six Figures? Not Enough!" *New York Times* (February 27, 2005).

Quote on investment bankers making $600,000: Brooke Kroeger, "Feeling Poor on $600,000 a Year," *New York Times* (April 26, 1987).

Statistic of 1 in 100 Americans accumulating $1 million: Internal Revenue Service, "Personal Wealth: Top Wealth Holders with Net Worth of $1 Million or More, 1998."

Information on private banking categories: Robert Frank, "Rich, Richer, Richest: Private Banks' Class System," *Wall Street Journal* (September 8, 2004).

Quote from *Forbes* article: Joe Queenan, "Billionaire Blues," *Forbes* (October 6, 2003).

Wall Street Journal article on yacht competition: Robert Frank, "Making Waves: New Luxury Goods Set Super-Wealthy Apart from Pack," *Wall Street Journal* (December 14, 2004).

Journalist's mission to figure out the cafe crowd: Erika Kinetz, "Here's to the Loafers Who Lunch," *New York Times* (April 17, 2005).

Jamie Johnson's documentary on children of wealth: *Born Rich* (Shout Factory, 2004).

Quote from Margaret Mead: Margaret Mead, *And Keep Your Powder Dry: An Anthropologist Looks at America* (New York: W. Morrow and Co., 1942).

For more about the challenges of wealth and inheritances, see: Thayer Cheatham Willis, *Navigating the Dark Side of Wealth: A Life Guide for Inheritors* (Portland, OR: New Concord Press, 2003); Jessie O'Neill, *The Golden Ghetto: The Psychology of Affluence* (Milwaukee: The Affluenza Project, 1997); Eileen Gallo and Jon Gallo, *Silver Spoon Kids: How Successful Parents Raise Responsible Children* (Chicago: Contemporary Books, 2002).

Quotes from Jessie O'Neill: O'Neill, *Golden Ghetto*.

Anecdotes from therapist in Manhattan: Donna Laikind, personal interview.

Quote from anthology's footnote to the "Richard Cory" poem: William Harmon, *The Top 500 Poems* (New York: Columbia University Press, 1992), 887.

Line from Simon and Garfunkel song: "Richard Cory," *Sounds of Silence* (Columbia Records, 1966).

Discussion of equity theory: Robert A. Baron and Donn Erwin Byrne, *Social Psychology: Understanding Human Interaction* (Boston: Allyn and Bacon, 1991), 626.

Experiment with three sets of office workers: R.D. Pritchard, M.D., Dunnette and D.O. Jorgenson, "Effects of Perceptions of Equity and Inequality on Worker Performance and Satisfaction," *Journal of Applied Psychology* 56, no. 1 (1972): 75–94. Summarized in *Social Psychology*, cited above.

Definition of mammon by a scholar and quote from Ronald Nash on the camel and eye of the needle passage: Ronald Nash, "What Is Money?" published on the Internet, www.apuritansmind.com/Stewardship/Nash RonaldWhatIsMoney.htm (accessed March 28, 2005).

Quote from inheritor/social worker comparing welfare people and inheritors: Mark McDonough, quoted in Stephen Dubner, "Suddenly Popular," *New York Times Magazine* (June 8, 2003): 68.

Quotes from Thayer Willis about inheritors going out on their own: Willis, *Dark Side of Wealth*.

Examples of how to answer the question of "What do you do?": "What Do You Do?" *More than Money* (December 1993).

Anecdote and quote from the Portland money doctor about the inheritor in his thirties: Willis, *Dark Side of Wealth*.

Quote from Margaret Mead regarding ladder climbers: Mead, *Keep Your Powder Dry*.

Quotes from *Born Rich* and Johnson and the map dealer: the documentary *Born Rich* cited above.

Quote from social psychology textbook about working: Baron and Byrne, *Social Psychology*.

Quote from Jessie O'Neill on not having to work being terrifying: Michelle Goldberg, "Crying All the Way to the Bank: Trust-Fund Babies of the World Are Uniting to Share Their Secret Pain," Salon.com (October 29, 1997).

Chapter Seven: Conclusion

Information and quote from the book on marathon training: David A. Whitsett, Forrest A. Dolgener, and Tanjala Mabon Kole, *The Non-Runner's Marathon Trainer* (Chicago: Masters Press, 1998).

For more on the practice of using your mind to change reality, see Napoleon Hill's *Think and Grow Rich!* (San Diego, CA: Aventine Press, 2004).

Quote from Abraham Lincoln: www.quotationspage.com/quotes/Abraham_Lincoln.

New York Times Magazine article on Buddhist meditation: Stephen S. Hall, "Is Buddhism Good for Your Health?" *New York Times Magazine* (September 14, 2003): 46–49.

For more information on Jon Kabat-Zinn's meditation class (Mindfulness-Based Stress Reduction) and to find a local course, refer to the Center for Mindfulness at the University of Massachusetts Medical School, www.umassmed.edu/cfm/.

Quote from Thoreau on the hurry and waste of life: Henry David Thoreau, *Walden* (1854).

Cadillac's "The Penalty of Leadership" ad: *Saturday Evening Post*, January 2, 1915. Full text accessible online at www.cadillacforums.com/cadillac/penalty1.html.

Quote from advertising professor James Twitchell: personal interview.

Quote from Rolex ad: Roy H. Williams, *The Wizard of Ads: Turning Words into Magic and Dreamers into Millionaires* (Austin, TX: Bard Press, 1998), 28–29.

Quote from social psychology textbook on downward comparison: Douglas T. Kenrick, Steven L. Neuberg, and Robert B. Cialdini, *Social Psychology: Unraveling the Mystery*, third edition (Boston: Allyn and Bacon, 2005), 83.

Discussion of exchange networks in poorer communities: Katherine Newman, *Falling from Grace: The Experience of Downward Mobility in the American Middle Class* (New York: Vintage Books, 1989).

Quote from the thesaurus, attributed to Samuel Miller: Marc McCutcheon, *Roget's Super Thesaurus*, second edition (Cincinnati, OH: Writer's Digest Books, 1998), 146.

Rabbi talking about loving yourself before your neighbor: Benjamin Blech, *Taking Stock: A Spiritual Guide to Rising above Life's Financial Ups and Downs* (New York: AMACOM, 2003), 28.

Quote from Jerrold Mundis's book based on Debtors Anonymous: *How to Get Out of Debt, Stay Out of Debt & Live Prosperously* (New York: Bantam Books, 1990), 58.

Endnotes

Quote from Cornelius Vanderbilt about having nothing to strive for: Williams, *Wizard of Ads*, 154.

Anecdote and quote about money coming from where it is right now: Deepak Chopra, *Creating Affluence: The A-to-Z Steps to a Richer Life* (San Rafael, CA: Amber-Allen Publishing and New World Library, 1993), 58.

Studies on the benefits of confession summarized and reported in James W. Pennebaker, Cheryl F. Hughes, and Robin C. O'Heeron, "The Psychophysiology of Confession: Linking Inhibitory and Psychosomatic Processes," *Journal of Personality and Social Psychology* 52, no. 4 (April 1987): 781–793.

Quote from anthropologist Margaret Mead: Margaret Mead, *And Keep Your Powder Dry: An Anthropologist Looks at America* (New York: W. Morrow and Co., 1942).

Suggested Resources

Personal Finance Books I Have Found Most Helpful

Financial Peace, by Dave Ramsey. An easy read, in the step-by-step guide-book style. It includes interesting and helpful sections about sales techniques and negotiation tactics among other tidbits to get your financial life in order.

How to Get Out of Debt, Stay Out of Debt & Live Prosperously, by Jerrold Mundis. To me, this book is a page-turner. It explains the steps and principles of the Debtors Anonymous program, but you don't have to be a big debtor to benefit from the storytelling and strategies given.

The 9 Steps to Financial Freedom, by Suze Orman. Along with nuts-and-bolts advice, Orman delves into financial psychology and the meaningfulness of money in life.

A Random Walk Down Wall Street, by Burton Malkiel. This is the book that stockbrokers don't want you to have. If you want to understand investing in the stock market, this is what you need to know. It shows why we should be broadly indexing rather than investing in a portfolio of individual stocks or managed mutual funds.

Smart Women Finish Rich, by David Bach. Even for couples, I always recommend this original volume. Although I don't agree with every bit of financial advice Bach puts forward, the book is a motivator and includes incredibly useful sections on setting and achieving goals (the techniques he uses are adapted from life coach Anthony Robbins).

Think and Grow Rich!, by Napoleon Hill. This self-help guide from the 1930s has a cult following among super-driven people. It's another endorsement of brain power and using perspective to your advantage.

Other Resources That Have Influenced *Green with Envy*

The Non-Runner's Marathon Trainer, by David Whitsett, Forrest Dolgener, and Tanjala Kole. Trains your mind to tackle any challenge and shows how to exert more control over your life.

The Seven Spiritual Laws of Success, by Deepak Chopra. A primer on how to consciously create your best life.

What the Bleep Do We Know!? An engrossing, truly mind-bending documentary that explores, among other topics, how we can consciously affect physical reality. If the principles of the marathon training program or of Chopra's book intrigue you, this serves as an advanced course that explains how they work on the level of quantum physics.

Index

Index